Culture Up

HOW STARTUPS SUCCEED BY
PUTTING PEOPLE FIRST

– The Future is Human-Centric –

Mareike Mutzberg
& Margareta Sailer

D1470681

© Mareike Mutzberg & Margareta Sailer 2022

Published by Orchard Publishing Consultancy

A catalogue record for this book is available from the British Library

ISBN 978-1-9162861-4-6 E-Book
ISBN 978-1-9162861-5-3 (Pbk)

Inside designed by xhtdesign
Cover design and Chapter artwork Frau Selig Grafikdesign

A Message from the Authors

Before you start to read this book, we have a message for you, which is close to our hearts.

Our world, this wonderful pale blue dot as Carl Sagan described it, is in dire need of protection. Therefore, sustainability is key. There are many startups with a vision to save the world and with a mission to do so by reducing waste, fishing it out of the ocean, recycling differently, saving CO_2 and so on.

But Startups often struggle with funding, finding the right partners, suppliers and achieving a supportive network. So, many great and potentially world-saving ideas never get realised because the startup simply didn't take off.

We've seen many times that startups with a strong founding or core team were more likely to attract investors, who in return would introduce them to the right suppliers and partners and even vouched for them.

With a strong initial core team behind you, you are more likely to believe in yourself and draw energy from it when presenting, and selling, your idea to investors, Business Angels or Venture Capitalists (VCs).

So, this book starts exactly here: how you start and maintain a great team in a truly inspiring culture. We want to give you a head start so your ideas flourish and you can leave your mark on this world.

Margareta Sailer & Mareike Mutzberg

Contents

BEFORE YOU START

The Importance of People

Why are people your most important asset?

When humans lived in caves, nothing was possible without the tribe. The tribe had one common goal: survive to thrive. Every individual had to contribute or be excluded, and exclusion meant certain death.

Times have moved on, but we still need our tribe. And your company is, or will be, a tribe of like-minded people with one common goal. The goal is to survive as a company, thrive in business and fulfil its purpose. So, the goal of the tribe comes from you. As the founder, the original goal is your goal. It is your tribe you brought together, under your vision. So, it is also your responsibility to keep it together under a common culture. You are the cultural leader.

Your company's survival depends on it.

Very soon most of us will probably be commuting to work in a self-driving car, by hyperloop or bullet train or maybe by air taxi, if we go to work at all – in the traditional sense. Our homes will be fully automated, and even the diagnostics and medicines that treat our ailments will likely be driven by Artificial Intelligence (AI).

But we will still be deeply human, with all our faults, foibles and sensitivities. The successful leader of the future in our AI driven world will be the leader who recognises that human emotions, reactions, responses and relationships will still be the driving force that brings these new technologies to market and keeps them running smoothly behind the scenes.

Understanding people, understanding yourself, knowing what drives us, excites us and gives us meaning and purpose will become a key component of being successful in a world where so many current task based jobs are being replaced by AI (in contrast to relationship based ones).

When one understands what drives us and what we are good at, we will find a way to make a mark on this world.

But let's be honest about it. It's the founders, the leaders, and the visionaries like you, who are most likely to put in the sustained effort and do the challenging thinking that's required to build and grow a highly functioning team. Many of the people you will lead and manage will expect you to lead from the front and explore the way ahead first.

It is incumbent upon you to create an environment where people can develop and see opportunities to learn new things. It's up to you to give people permission to fail, and then try again. It's not easy, but it is possible, to use your emotional intelligence to create environments where people feel heard, connected, acknowledged and being part of something bigger than themselves – because that is what will make your company succeed in the end.

It's more important than ever for you to develop what AI can't do yet which is to listen, show empathy, solve conflicts, be creative and make teamwork happen.

Soft skills do not depend on intelligence alone, but on your emotional intelligence (EQ – Emotional Quotient).

Over time, you will create and develop your personal values; things like fairness, respect and reliability, to work on your personal traits, such as serenity, patience and kindness and to work on your skills, things like critical ability, listening skills, boundary setting, assertiveness and conflict management. To lead your startup to success, you will need to continually upgrade your social abilities, deal with other people, encourage teamwork, and develop your empathy and communication skills.

As Dr Georg Wolfgang, founder and CEO of Culturizer GmbH,

which is helping to develop culture for companies professionally, put it:

'*We are missing a metric to translate team & culture from expectation to reality and hoist this topic out of the soft skill swamp onto the solid ground of fact.*'

These things are often labelled 'soft skills', yet we don't believe that name is helpful because some people think that the term 'soft' implies that those things aren't as important as 'hard' skills which are financial, technical and specialist knowledge. The very term implies that those who focus on them are weak and not business like. Don't be fooled by fluffy terminology! In fact, in order to avoid any misconception, nowadays, soft skills are also known as power or human skills.

We like the word power skills!

The simple fact is that hard skills alone don't get anyone far. Unless you can influence people and have the personal skills to self-manage in a sustainable way, you're unlikely to cope well with the rigours of being a founder. Power skills are vital both for you and everyone around you. People will look to you as a role model for *How Things Are Done Around Here*. Much of what they see will be your power skill set. People will evaluate and even copy your personal traits. They'll observe and look to you as a role model of how to do lots of things; how you cope with stress, how you treat people and how you manage yourself. You are a leader now, so don't let the 'soft' skills label put you off or trick you into thinking they don't matter as much as having a great product. Developing them is vital for your leadership and the success of your company.

We've seen many times that startups with a strong founding team and a great vision are more likely to attract investors, who in return could, and were willing to, introduce them to the right suppliers and partners who then vouched for the startup.

The people you choose to surround yourself with are vital.

With a strong initial core team behind you, you can push further. Draw energy and inspiration from a diverse group of people, those with experience and those who like to further themselves and the company. It will help you to create a more even rounded product and allows for a more compelling story to potential investors.

We want to give you a head start so your idea flourishes and you can leave your mark on this world. We don't want to deep dive into grey theory and strategy but rather give you a good experience-based baseline for the beginning. So, buckle UP and read on to find out how.

CULTURE

Culture is in everything we do.
It is part of our core as an individual
and as a group of people.
Culture connects us.

1.1 What and Why

Building a Solid Foundation

In our mentoring group for founders, one startup mentor shared with us a story of his mentee, Thomas. Thomas' proposition was to develop and distribute a sustainable bicycle and skateboard line. But Thomas had a history with startups. And it wasn't great. His story shows the pitfalls of dealing with the company mission and leaving the 'soft' stuff to chance.

Thomas was in his mid 30's. He'd already founded three other companies but they had all failed. So, for his new idea, he looked for a mentor for help. Everything looked promising; his market research, potential funding, the business plan and the strategy: all appeared solid.

Our mentor friend asked Thomas what went wrong with his previous businesses. Thomas told him, 'My first startup was about creating a management tool for garbage disposal companies to improve the recycling process. It only lasted five months. I had an MBA and my co-founder was a programmer. When we looked for the people with skills we needed, we couldn't agree on anything, let alone on candidates – even if they were only short term or freelancers! We argued a lot and had to stop our startup before it had really begun.'

His second startup he founded alone. His idea was programming a platform and App that supported healthier sustainable shopping choices and a plastic free lifestyle. He raised enough money through crowdfunding and angel investments to hire his first employees, but within two years that went down the drain as well. His small team fell apart. One woman quit because she had an argument with a workmate and couldn't get past it. The atmosphere soured and his neatly planned budget and timeline ran out. Thomas fell into a personal crisis. He didn't want to continue working on the project with these people. He'd had enough.

After a bit of time out, and a year later, he was asked by two friends to join their team of founders and he was ready for another startup challenge. The social networking platform grew to around twenty people, when yet again, Thomas started to sense tension within the team. A once positive atmosphere was replaced by friction between co-workers. People started to avoid each other. He overheard conversations in the kitchen, 'I don't know why we spend so much time on this to be honest/ This is frustrating/I'm applying for jobs/I really don't need to be continuously questioned about everything.'

The founders and senior team were blissfully unaware until then. He knew from bitter experience that the team was falling apart, but he had no idea what to do about it. Again, the company failed.

Now, with his sustainable bicycle and skateboard line, he had one more try. But this time, he knew it had to work so, he signed up for the mentoring programme. Exploring past failures in detail with his mentor, Thomas realised that every failure was down to at least team and culture issues. So, they started looking at how to get it right this time. From day one, they paid much more attention to recruiting, onboarding, team building, personal development, corporate culture, internal communications and leadership.

Thomas recalled 'I had always put those soft skills areas aside and didn't take them seriously enough. There were more tangible things to take care of like funding and product validation, and I think I assumed these side issues, as I saw them, would somehow grow naturally in time. If I had thought about it actively for a minute, I would have seen the obvious. It is one of the most important things you have to take care of as soon as you have employees.'

For his fourth startup, he recruited a co-founder, with a good cultural and values fit. Together they have actively developed a 'people first' culture where the team can grow together. He's still in business after four years.

Thomas told us that nowadays he follows a simple, yet powerful mantra: take care of others, and they will take care of you.

Let's focus on how you can help yourself and your startup when it comes to recruitment, people management and communication. Hint: first and foremost create a strong company culture. Please see example on page 256.

Company Culture

So, what is company culture? Company culture, also often known as organisational culture, is a set of shared values, norms, rituals and beliefs which influence how the people behave, make decisions, act, and communicate. In other words, it's how they work, collaborate, interact with your suppliers and customers and how they feel about themselves and their role in your company. In essence, culture is simply *How We Do Things and How We Treat People Around Here.*

When people think of company culture, they often think of free food, football tables, and bean bags. But to be very clear: those are just the working environment, which supports and partly reflects your culture, but that's it. Culture is often invisible but people feel it and respond to it either positively or negatively.

Arnnon Geshuri is the former CHRO of Tesla and current CPO of Teladoc, who joined Google in 2004 when the company had just emerged from its IPO and he helped scale the company from 2,500 employees to rapidly evolve into a 25,000 person technology powerhouse.

We asked Arnnon what advice he would give to any entrepreneur who wants to start a business.

His response to us was, 'Know the purpose of your company. What changes will it make in the world? Focus on how you differentiate your culture and especially your mission from others. What makes you unique? A clearly defined culture will be, in part, how you attract talent. Being able to tell a clear story about your company and its impact and values will help you find the right people who will align with it.

It is essential to think carefully about the first few people that you hire, from founders to initial staff. What are your expectations for the people who will work for you? Get advice from the original people you took on in various areas of expertise. Often these people will help you to avoid problems and you will move faster. Listen to great ideas from your folks. If you hire well, you should feel confident enough to listen to them. Be involved in all aspects of the company but don't micromanage.'

In short, know your purpose, create a good environment and communicate well with people so that they know your mission. If you miss this, it's not going to be enjoyable, and you will miss the magic of a uniting, mission driven culture.

Why is it Important?

When Shawn and Matt decided to set up their online trading startup they thought that they had thought everything through.

Everything was neatly planned and laid out in lots of paperwork. They even had a personnel plan for the next six months with basic guidelines for their hiring process. Then the day came, when their first two employees arrived to start work.

'We bought some sandwiches and juice, made coffee and organised a little welcome meeting for them. But we weren't prepared at all for what came next,' Shawn told me.

'We showed them their desks, where everything was prepared, from laptop to paper clip and they started working.

After a while the questions came flying towards us.

> What was the guideline on how to work with customers?
>
> Who should take care of the info@address inbox?
>
> Did we want them to use a headed letter template for formal communication?
>
> When it comes to company communication, is WhatsApp or Slack used?
>
> When it comes to holiday, does an employee have to make a formal request, and does this also apply to having to leave early?
>
> What was the policy for lunch breaks?
>
> And most important, who was their direct report?

The list of questions went on.

The new team members had also started storing documents in their own folder structures or on their desktop which meant nobody could share knowledge, never mind the data privacy and IT risks it caused.

We quickly realised that we had completely neglected having a solid onboarding structure as part of our company culture. People needed to know how to collaborate and communicate with each other online, and offline, said Matt.

We showed them how the two of us had collaborated so far, but they challenged us on everything, questioned our logic and suggested 'more efficient' ways of doing things. They meant well, but with one of them, it escalated and affected our personal relationships.

We didn't mind the ideas of improvement at all, it was more the communication style and persistence that things needed to be done their way, that bothered us.

In the end, one of those first two employees quit after only five weeks while the other, a software developer, turned out to be a lucky find in the sense that he was a true generalist with a solution-oriented mindset.

He was eager to solve problems and not leave anything to chance with future colleagues. He put the company values, vision and mission statement in writing, drafted policies and guidelines for collaboration, wrote down some basic, and necessary processes and structures that allowed for collaboration, and created the most basic templates.

We all had a discussion and agreed it was the best we could do for now; we needed to keep things simple and review them every six months.

In short, this employee had set up our basic company culture and it allowed us to improve the onboarding experience for every hire after that dramatically.

Nevertheless, this lesson was an expensive one and it really cut a hole in our budget. But now we have the saying: better hobbling away with a lesson learned than going down with the flag waving.'

The story above is not a single event, but rather a normal situation for a young startup. Company culture is a very powerful thing – in fact, it has the power to make or break your startup.

Mind the Startup Person

Believe it or not, your company's culture even has the power to shape your people's personal view of the world. Everyone tends to identify with their job, which gives them a certain social status in society, think of a lawyer's or doctor's reputation. And then there is a certain pride in being part of a small startup, in being a 'startup person'.

When you come across a startup person, you cannot underestimate that feeling of pride in being the disruptor, the underdog, that feeling of 'us against the world'. It's incredibly important for these people to know what they are fighting for, what exactly they are part of, what culture they are in, which sets the boundaries for how they will behave. So, by forming an initial culture, you make it easier for them to identify with it, thrive in it, and to embrace a new purpose in life. Culture is a big part of keeping people happy and engaged which gives them purpose. You must not underestimate this. You're not simply giving them bread on the table, but, more importantly, giving them something to strive for and a reason to get up in the morning.

Benefits

What are the benefits of establishing a company culture early?

When you are starting out, you cannot compete with the Big Boys, you can't offer the perks and often you will not be able to match the salaries and associated benefits.

But you still want to attract the best people. You need the creative, resourceful and entrepreneurial minds who will help you get your company off the ground. Over the first two to five years you will need those intrinsically motivated people who believe that your product or service has a space in this world even if everyone else is laughing at your idea. You need those 'startup people'.

Your culture will help you define your employer brand.

It is a crowded employer market and candidates can pick and choose.

Whether you are looking for candidates who are actively looking for a job, or those you need to convince to leave another job to join you, it is not just the product or mission, moreover it's your culture and team which will attract them.

Research from Glassdoor has shown that 79% of all candidates research your company culture before they apply for a job. Your culture is your unique selling point (USP) and will set you apart from other companies in your industry sector. It is in fact the crucial element to attract talent.

Winifred Patricia Johansen, VP of Commercial Affairs for Quantafuel, and an authority on Diversity, shared with us how companies, from startups to large corporations can ensure that they have a thriving and successful company and culture.

'And here is the thing, by defining your company culture early on, it will attract people who can see themselves in many of your values which means they will make an immediate impact. Your employee engagement level will be higher from day one, because you know that the people you hired associate with your company or product immediately.

Suppliers and partners will seek you out not just for your product, but because your company values align with their own. As a result, you already have a common ground and language with which to do business.'

Your culture will help with the day to day business, in other words to align and unite the team towards one common goal and purpose.

We cannot emphasise enough the importance of taking the time and effort to define your culture. The wording of each cultural statement or your perspective on certain aspects might change in the future, but everything should be consistent and one you stand behind, 100% personally.

The second most important thing is to get it 'out there'! State it boldly on your website, post it on social media regularly – maybe post short stories or repost, like and share third party content, which hits home for you. Take part in competitions, or be seen at fairs, give speeches at events etc. which represent your values. For example, send your female staff to women-in-tech events and conferences representing your company or send in your business case to a startup sustainability contest – and even if you don't win, talk about it! Connect your external communication to your vision, your mission and values... whatever you do, be seen and make your culture known.

It helps networking, finding suitable investors as well as mentors.

Winifred Johansen told us, that she frequently hears from Venture Capitals (VCs) who are looking to invest in diverse teams or startups run by minorities, or those tackling health, social, environmental problems.

More and more they are actively searching for flagship startups to support which they can shine with. What almost all VC's have in common, though, is that they are looking for startups with strong core teams, a strong vision and mission and sustainability as a core value.

Having a clear culture and communicating it, increases your chances of attracting specialised VCs and investors who are specialised in supporting the kind of startup you have – Win, Win!

Culture enables retention and loyalty.

Internally, culture touches, or better, wraps around everything.

Without a clearly defined culture, you cannot communicate properly, because without a clear plan behind it such as which tone of voice to use with which channel and what exactly to say to whom and when, it would all be random. To give you an idea of what we mean, one day you might feel like communicating a decision about a new tool to your IT department, but the next day, you might not feel like communicating something about a new partner to your marketing and communications team. However, they would have needed to know about it in order to prepare a timely press release. This might sound like an over-dramatic example but take a minute to think about other implications which having no culture could mean for communication, collaboration and team spirit.

We had an interesting conversation with Paula Leach, formerly Chief People Office for the Home Office in the UK, and Winifred Patricia Johansen on the topic of leadership and culture. Both stated that what matters most, was to think about your culture as early as possible. Everything interlinks when it comes to the type of culture you create, either consciously or subconsciously.

On top of that, Paula Leach believes that the success of the human race was based on innovation, creativity and socialisation. Over the decades we have turbocharged this, through globalisation.

If you want to excel at this, you need to understand human behaviour and how to create the best environments and cultures which are about feeling and being, as much as doing.

A culture of ownership and accountability will focus on delivery and results.

We asked Boryana Straubel, the late Bulgarian businesswoman, founder of the Straubel Foundation and ex Tesla Exec about her experience in what sets successful startups apart with regards to culture?

Those startups which are very successful, often provide a work environment that is meaningful; it's where people identify with the vision and mission of the company, making it an exciting enjoyable place to work.

Foster collaboration across all levels, allow individuals to be themselves and speak up to enable diversity of thought to create the best possible product.

It will inspire your people's private life as well – and it will snowball further.

Your company's culture is a source of inspiration for your people, as it has the power to change their personal lives.
Mareike Mutzberg

By inspiring your team members to do the right thing, which your culture should be all about, they inevitably will be mindful about those things in their private lives too and carry it through to their family and friends.

In this way you can make use of free advertising for your cause and culture – and your company – through the 'snowball-effect'.

──────── **Mareike shares a personal example** ────────

In Germany, recycling waste is a high priority and upcycling is also a popular thing. A friend of mine, who had been born and raised in India and studied in Germany, hadn't come across this concept before and took an interest in it. He told his family in Mumbai all about what was going on and how the company he worked for even took it to the next level by having an 'environmental lunch' every Friday, where employees were encouraged to discuss ideas to minimize, reuse and upcycle waste. This conversation inspired his mother and aunt to start upcycling things as well, like making arty watering cans out of lemonade bottles and mosaic artwork out of broken mirrors. What started out as a local idea spread way beyond borders. The great side effect was that now a whole village in India was talking about the company my friend was working for.

1.2 How to Set It up?

How is Company Culture Formed?

Just like babies are born with an individual personality already, your company will have an inherent culture right from the start. The way you all work and collaborate, how you treat partners, suppliers, customers and investors, what you value and what you strive for... your behaviour, your beliefs, the way you act, think and talk... all this forms your company's identity; its culture. So, if your company is 'born' with one, why not nurture and form it actively right from the start just like you would raise your child? You can always change culture at a later stage, but this will then be a whole change management project. This will be a lot harder, time consuming and costly as you need to consider all processes, systems and documents not to mention getting your people on board which, in reality, is always the hardest part. It takes a lot of sensitivity, planning and convincing and still it most likely causes frustration, friction, even with people quitting and the resultant loss of productivity.

And then there is THE startup culture

Startups automatically bring a unique culture. Maybe you are one of those 'Startup people' yourself. Startup people have an entrepreneurial drive and simply cannot envision themselves working for a big company. If you are a startup person then you know of the inherent startup atmosphere, and when you imagine walking into the office of a startup, you can see, smell, hear, feel the 'startup vibes'.

So, when you found a company, you will benefit from this

inherent startup culture, which attracts a certain type of talent; the startup person, the builder, the dreamer and believer. Leverage your talent and build on it.

If you want to know what exactly makes a startup culture special, here are the four key factors that shape it and make it a unique place to work:

PASSION

Almost all startups start out as the underdog. You don't have a big name, you are unlikely able to pay much salary, but your culture and your passion for the cause is the thing which drives people into your company. For your team, it doesn't feel like work, but rather like a secret mission into which they put all their effort, time and dedication. Celebrate your team's success, harness that energy.

IDENTITY

Startup people need to identify themselves with the startup they work in. So, what is your company's personality, what's its USP? The very first people in your team will automatically feel strongly connected with you and your company and stand behind your cause. Make use of this feeling of belonging and pride and carry it with you for as long as you can.

AGILITY

Knowledge and experience flow easily through all areas of your company, which increases productivity and efficiency. One benefit of a small company is that everybody is still working closely together, they are connected and still talking to each other. Plus, there isn't too much knowledge to manage yet, so what's there can be shared with everybody easily. This makes it easy in the beginning to align and focus the team on your goals and to foster a growth mindset.

Furthermore, you don't have too many goals to reach yet, you probably have only one product or one service so you can focus and be very agile about that one thing. Make use of that efficiency and focus.

AUTHENTICITY

It's about the freedom and the respect for the individual personality of each team member. Everybody still knows everyone personally. This true bond between team members allows everyone to be authentic and to be true to themselves, which creates a feeling of safety, belonging and self-respect. That keeps motivation high and will endure through hard times. Bigger companies have very strict processes and clear hierarchies, in which everyone has to play a role, which might not always reflect their true personality, which drains energy and motivation. A startup is exactly the opposite. You're free to make decisions and you can have real impact. Make use of that truly human centred approach.

If you're able to nurture and foster these traits, you will carry that forward when you set up your culture more formally and develop it further. How? With the help of your cultural co-founders, your initial team.

―――――――――――――――― **David's story** ――――――――――――――――

David, founder of a software-as-a-service startup, told me that his first employee was a good friend and they worked well together. They understood each other, trusted each other implicitly, and supported and complemented each other almost perfectly. The second employee wasn't known to the team or their network. She was hired using the company's official application process. She brought all the required skills for the job, and on a personal note, David could see himself working with her every day. He described it as 'there was a connection right from the start' and that it was a 'gut feeling to hire her'.

In the turbulent times of a very fresh startup, his first two employees met each other for the first time at a business event. David needed all six hands on deck to present his startup and win B2B clients and find suppliers. He only realised when they introduced themselves to each other on the first morning of the fair, that he should have been more prepared and he should have introduced them to each other properly. Maybe he should have involved his first employee in the recruitment in the first place. What if they didn't get along? They would have to work very closely together so this could be a disaster. Luckily David's gut feeling had been right and his first two employees got on very well.

> If you can laugh together, you can work together.
> Robert Orben

Empowering Your Team

So how do you set about developing your team?

Elena, co-founder and CEO of a consultancy startup for female entrepreneurs, shared a personal learning with us:

'In the beginning, it was hard for me not to micromanage. It was my company, my heart, my dream, my money which was at stake should something go wrong. I was tempted to control every decision taken, whether two comparison offers from different suppliers had been asked for, whether my employees treated our customers, partners and suppliers in the way I wanted them to, whether our timeline was kept up to date and if we were still on track with everything. How could I make sure my employees understood what was expected from them and felt about this company as I did without dictating every single step? In the end, my co-founders and I decided to search for mentors. We would *have one each, so we had different perspectives to compare and combine and the path became clear; we needed to develop a culture and involve our team.'*

The co-founders took time to write down their vision, mission and purpose statements and then called for a 'Culture Day', inviting every team member to participate and create their culture together based on their newly introduced culture statements.

This culture team decided that they would not identify explicit values and write them in stone yet, but rather write an open culture letter, where they set out what was important to them all and how they wanted to work together.

From that letter, they identified seven 'Golden Rules', which they hung up in the main office as a poster.

THE 7 GOLDEN RULES

1. **Communicate** – be clear, concise and coherent, put everything in writing (meeting agenda, purpose, outcome and decisions, next steps, responsible persons etc.)
2. **Share your resources** – tools, manhours and knowledge
3. **Respect each other** – treat each other as you want to be treated, follow but also challenge your leader; coach, enable and guide your subordinates. Have an open mind, learn from each other
4. **No ego** – flat hierarchy, take responsibility for your actions and reflect to self-correct
5. **Be punctual** – for meetings, for deadlines, for communication
6. **Solve problems** – for the company and for each other, keep cultural differences in mind, address conflicts openly and with the intent to resolve them constructively
7. **Give feedback** – tell others what went well and what you suggest improving looking beyond your scope of work

Six months later, when the team had locked in the first Seed funding round and had hired another ten people, Elena and her co-founders organised another culture day, where they reviewed if what they had established worked for them or needed adjusting.

'We didn't have to change much, there were only some misconceptions due to ambiguous wording here and there, which were refined. We agreed that we were at a stage where we needed dedicated principles for meetings and feedback, which went beyond the scope of our Golden Rules. Then we celebrated our culture with a night out in town with the whole team. It felt like a huge milestone was reached and the celebration made it somehow official.'

Elena told me, that the next day, the team started signing their names underneath the wall display of the Seven Golden Rules. That moment, she knew, she could let go and trust that her employees would come to her with any issue which was not resolvable by following the principles of the Golden Rules.

First Employees

Make your first employees your cultural co-founders

Dr Georg Wolfgang (Culturizer GmbH) shared with us his experience:

'Taking time for the development of your team and your culture is absolutely essential for your success.

It will be an ongoing process; never stop thinking about it, never stop developing and facilitating conversations, ideas and teamwork. If you don't, the team will inevitably develop in directions which are, most of the time, not beneficial.

In our experience, there is a magic threshold at around thirty employees or – if the team stays small – twelve months. Until then, you can create, form, establish, initiate, try out, introduce, challenge and change everything easily and mostly with the acceptance and support of your team. After that, the system for how to collaborate, interact and behave is set and difficult to change. So, I strongly recommend using that period to do exactly that; create, form and establish your team and corporate culture – and do involve your team!'

Going back to David and his narrow escape. His gut feeling had been right and his two first employees did get along very well. But what if they hadn't? He decided not to leave this to chance with future colleagues and sought out the help of a friend who worked as head of recruiting at a textile company. They sat down and identified how his 'gut feeling' translated into values, which he could hire against:

Integrity

Teamwork

Ownership

Passion

Open Mindedness.

They also talked about what David wanted the hiring and onboarding process to look like, and his friend helped with further ideas and things to consider from her experience. It was simply a friendly talk over a glass of wine not a professional consultation, but it had helped him get on his feet and gave him a rough plan of what to do next. He involved his two employees in his plan and together they created a solid recruiting basis, which all three of them could stand behind.

Now, they had the framework to help them select the 'cultural fit' of all future applicants, who would own their company's culture as much as they did. Happy Ending?

Well, I'd rather call it 'Lucky Ending', because it could have gone terribly wrong and cost David his startup before it had even taken off.

What could he do to prevent disharmony among his team? How could he make sure his employees were collaborating in an effective and beneficial way? David didn't know, so he simply asked them again. Together, they agreed on five habits that would help them collaborate efficiently and effectively as a team. They would review them together on a regular basis and evaluate how well they were serving them and if they needed updating.

HABITS

1 Deliver: better done than perfect but unfinished

2 Credit: give credit where credit is due

3 Challenge: question the status quo and speak up

4 Value: respect each other's time by being punctual and keeping deadlines; value and respect each other

5 Sharpen the saw: choose the right tools for your work

With this, David had made his first two employees *cultural co-founders*, who held a personal stake in the company culture. They felt it was *their* culture and would act as ambassadors and role models for future employees demonstrating, rather than dictating, what they had established together: which was their values and their habits. They were ready to take that knowledge and help new hires immerse themselves in, and add to, the company culture.

Meggy's story

Meggy will share her personal stories on the topic of culture.

They show what it means to people when you work within a company that communicates its culture clearly and consistently and one that does not.

Communicating company culture doesn't always mean writing things on the wall.

Most importantly it means consistent action from the leadership team to drive and live the culture across the company, regardless of its age or stage.

'Early in my career, I joined Blackberry during its expansion phase. Having worked in a company that felt like it scaled faster than the speed of light at the time, I would say that Blackberry never really had a clearly defined company culture. Looking back, the feeling of working within this company was completely different from how I felt I when recruiting and working for companies like Tesla or Lilium.

In retrospect it's astounding how much more purposeful, and mission driven, people were at Tesla or Lilium. That did not mean that we worked any less hard at BlackBerry, people worked incredibly hard at RIM. But when it came to culture, the feeling of togetherness and belonging, was really something that wasn't there. To me, BlackBerry felt more like a mix of very talented people that were all hired aggressively to get the products onto the market as quickly as possible.

Whereas, at Tesla and Lilium we hired new people fast with company culture in mind. We looked for certain attributes like the ability to solve problems, to work hard, and never give up as well as an ability to think creatively and be solution-oriented. We were ready to take on the world and show people what we were made of. We were 'cultural co-founders' and felt a deep ownership for what we did. We recruited people who had the intrinsic belief that the world as we know it had to change, and we were willing to make many personal sacrifices to do this. We all had the same goal and were driven by the same purpose. Spirits were high and we were ready to overcome all sorts of challenges simply because we had a common vision and mission and shared similar values.'

The Importance of Purpose

It's simple, Purpose drives everything from your company values to its goals.
Boryana Straubel
(Generation Collection & Straubel Foundation)

Or as Meggy would say: 'Purpose is about finding your passion, it's the very thing that keeps you going when things get tough. It can be like a magic pill that gets you out of bed in the morning and gets you excited.'

Purpose really is the reason that things exist. It drives Humans to invent, create and shape the great inventions of our time. Purpose gives us meaning, a path and goal.

As a Founder, C-Level executive leader you have your own personal drive and purpose, just like your teams have. And as for business, knowing your company's purpose is paramount to shaping and living the company's culture and succeeding as a team.

It's everyone's job to take an active part in bringing out the best in themselves through it. Therefore, they need to know why they are there and why they must do what they do. It doesn't stop there, think about your future board members, investors, partners and everyone in touch with your company. This is the most crucial one of the core cultural statements (vision, mission, values, purpose) at the beginning of your startup since it's the very reason for founding it in the first place. But it is not necessary to write it down and communicate it explicitly. Many companies include their purpose in their mission statement, which is absolutely fine since the mission should, after all, reflect the purpose – and in this way you will not confuse anyone with too many definitions.

Arnnon Geshuri told us that knowing your company's purpose will not just marry you and your employees towards the why, and help you through difficult times, but will also help you to share your vision with purpose.

He finds that the purpose is the fundamental anchor, it is the organisation's reason for existing and it ties into everything. Everything that your company does should be clearly connected to your purpose.

Customers purchasing behaviours are changing. Sure, price and quality always remain a big factor to your customers, but so are the values that your company stands for, including the purpose of the product and how it interacts with the world. How you source and produce your product and what it does to the world is becoming increasingly more of a concern to governments, leaders and your customers.

How to define your company's purpose

The truth is the purpose of your company should ideally exist in your head before you even founded it.

No matter what your personal reason is for founding a company – whether it be to financially secure your family, do something good, fix a problem in this world or simply become famous or rich, what most of all companies' purposes have in common, according to Dr Tina Ruseva, is the:

> **effort for efficiency; to be faster, better, doing things right.**

But doing things right has never been easier than nowadays in our AI (Artificial Intelligence) era, where information and software technology are enabling automation and with that an exponential increase in productivity. That means that we have never been more efficient. So, 'doing things right is a given' as Dr Ruseva states in her book Big Heart Ventures.

But our society is evolving too, and it is not only vital for our survival but also more acknowledged than ever that we need to think and act resourcefully, sustainably and put the environment in the centre. With that, our awareness of psychological, mental and physical wellbeing raises mindfulness. Mindfulness ties into meditation and human connection right back to ourselves, back to our roots, back to nature. We realise how much power lies within social connection, love and caring for each other and our world. Dr Tina Ruseva puts it: 'The time has now come to be doing the right things as well.'

With that in mind, how will your company be doing the right thing? What is its reason to exist? What do you want your company to stand for ethically, emotionally, historically and practically?

Your company's purpose is the driving force behind its truly perceived brand, no matter how you design or mask it, and it is maybe THE most critical aspect of your culture that creates your company's identity.

Cultural Statements

Defining your purpose was just the beginning. We bet that now you can picture what your overall company culture should look like, you know what it should feel like and maybe even have some phrases and definitions in your head already. But the question is, how can you translate your idea into something tangible and visual for every team member to know, absorb, live and refer to at any time?

The answer is simple. You pick the culture statements which resonate with your cultural idea, and then formulate and communicate them.

What are cultural statements?

Cultural statements are formulated claims, which depict your culture from various perspectives. They are there to enable your employees to do their jobs and help them understand what they can expect in return. No company is like any other and everyone has different requirements. But there are some basic cultural statements from which you can pick and choose as you see fit for your company.

Here are the most essential ones:

VISION STATEMENT

This is the cornerstone of your company and should have been there before you even founded it, at least as an image or dream you had. The vision statement describes how the world looks if your company is successful. Vision statements are aspirational. They are meant to inspire by painting a picture of a future worth working towards.

A good vision statement is short, simple, specific to your company and leaves nothing open to interpretation.

For example:

'Create economic opportunity for every member of the global workforce.' LinkedIn

MISSION STATEMENT

You know best how you want to reach your vision. So, make it a founder matter to formulate the mission statement. This is also a crucial element to have early on for defining and shaping your culture.

A mission statement is a guideline by which you operate. Everything you do as a company should work towards your mission.

For example:

'To organize the world's information and make it universally accessible and useful.' Google

PURPOSE

Again, your company's purpose should have been clear to you before you started. You can make it explicit in a written purpose statement, but most companies have included it in their mission statement. This is a 'nice to have' in an explicitly communicated way but it might only confuse people. The important thing is that you are clear on the purpose in your head.

For example:

'To work with others to overcome the obstacles that poverty, violence, disease and discrimination place in a child's path.' Unicef

VALUES

Every single person in your company has their own personal values. The ones that everyone in your company shares and agrees on are the ones driving the business by guiding the team to make decisions and behave correctly. Because they are such effective guidelines for the hiring process as well as a great figurehead for the outside world, it makes sense to make them explicit and communicate them in writing. Unlike the vision, mission and purpose of your company, the values might not exist in your head before founding your startup. They might have to ripen with your early team and develop before being outlined. Therefore, it makes sense to involve your initial team (the cultural co-founders) or even leave it to the experts in a dedicated department such as HR, Marketing, Communications or Public Relations.

For example: Coca Cola:

- **Leadership:** Have courage to shape a better future
- **Collaboration:** Leverage collective genius
- **Integrity:** Be real
- **Accountability:** If it is to be, it's up to me
- **Passion:** Committed in heart and mind
- **Diversity:** As inclusive as our brands
- **Quality:** What we do, we do well

Apart from the ones listed above, there are quite a few more possible culture statements and 'supporting statements' which support your culture rather than defining it and which you can choose from when the time is right or the need occurs.

- **Ways of Working**
- **Objectives**
- **Employee Handbook**
- **Code of Conduct**
- **Principles**
- **Policies**
- **Processes**
- **Manuals**
- **Workflows**
- **Guidelines**

Keep in mind that you might find different names for the elements (e.g. 'rules' can be another word for 'ways of working') but we tried to stick to the most common names used for these cultural/ supporting statements. You know how to use a search engine and if you're not sure which ones you need at which stage of your company and how to develop and implement them, consult with your mentors or feel free to contact us.

Creating your Cultural Statements

After reading this list of cultural and supporting statements, you should get a grasp of the abundance of elements you can choose from to define and stipulate your culture. You can see these as a buffet of cultural statements.

So how to do this. You can't simply lock yourself away and define the desirable culture. It needs to involve the small, intimate team of like-minded people you took on board first. All you need to do is involve them and allow them to become true cultural co-founders. Make this initial process transparent and open to everyone in the team. Your role as founder/CEO is to have a grasp of your options, which you have done now reading this chapter, and to make up your mind about your personal preferences and then moderate and steer the process, but you must refrain from dictating the outcome.

Give your team the freedom to go about the process in their own way. We met teams, who wanted to meet up regularly for a drink after work and discuss their culture. Others established a work force and asked for an hour a week for a couple of months. Yet others wrote their proposals on a whiteboard in the hallway so everyone could vote on the key ideas. Some wanted to establish values, others habits, again others 'the way we work' or the 'what we give and what we get-Manifesto'. Let your team be creative about what they want; support them, encourage them and participate yourself. After all, you as the founder must be content about the outcome and be satisfied with how your cultural statements look.

In general, less is more, especially in the early stages. You don't want to confuse people with the information overflow of a 'culture definition overkill'. Keep it short and simple. Pick as few as you can, which together present the essence of your company culture.

The majority of founders in various industries we asked recommend that you formally outline the following five elements in the early stages, which we talked about already:

The three main cultural statements:

1 **Vision**
2 **Mission, including purpose if suitable**
3 **Values**

Accompanied by the following supporting documents:

4 **Code of Conduct (consisting of the most essential policies)**
5 **Necessary processes including folder structures**

Everything else is a matter of personal preferences, the demands of the company or time. You, and later your division heads, will know whether it would make sense to introduce additional documents – and if so, when. If in doubt, ask your mentor or consultant to help you. Whatever you do, definitely do something, but don't overdo it!

A short note on the supporting documents. These documents don't primarily define or reflect your culture, like the cultural documents do, but they are essential to fix in place those rules and regulations, which support your culture.

We can tell you from experience, it will be a process – not something that happens in a day or a week. You might get a first draft done in a few hours, but it's normal for it to take months to reach a point where you are happy with each word that describes your culture.

Top Tip:

Throughout the book, we are going to share our personal Top Tips with you, which are based on our experience, sometimes even learned the hard way, thus, most of the time cannot be found in search machines. Make use of it, take the lead. And here is our first one.

Formulate your values as instructions instead of just presenting 'nice' nouns, it makes them far more actionable, for example, instead of just 'Kindness' write 'Treat everyone like you would like them to treat your mother'.

———————————————— Five steps ————————————————

Let's take the vision statement as an example. You will find many great manuals – and mentors – out there, both of which can help you with the others. We want to give you an idea of how to help yourself.

First of all, there are some basic guidelines you should follow which will differ from statement to statement. For the vision statement they will read:

- Keep it short and simple (maximum two sentences or thirty words)
- Make it aspirational, ambitious and inspiring, yet specific
- Make it relevant for your market
- Do not include numbers, dates or metrics
- Mind. Every. Single. Word.

1. MAKE A WORD CLOUD

Collect all the words that come to mind when you think of your company. Write them down, don't evaluate them yet. Just keep associating for a while. There are some free tools online, which you can use to create a word cloud automatically.

2. IMAGINE THE FUTURE
Imagine how the future will look with your company in it. What has changed because of it? What kind of impact did it have on the environment, society, architecture, infrastructure and so on?

3. FORMULATE A SENTENCE
Write down the most obvious sentence with your words and your inspiration. If there are more in your head, write more sentences down. This is a warmup and helps you avoid the blank page syndrome.

4. POLISH THE WORDS
Put your words and sentences away for a night and look at them with fresh eyes the following day. Now, choose the sentence which resonates with you the most. Is it complete or does it miss any important components of the other sentences you dismissed? Does it sound too vague? Add to it. Then look at every word. Do they hit home? If not, are there more suitable synonyms? Does it comply with your basic guidelines above?

5. INVOLVE YOUR TEAM (OR FRIENDS OR MENTORS)
If you're happy, introduce the draft of your vision statement to your team. If you don't have one yet, ask your circle of friends, family or mentors. Focus on the following questions:

- Is it understandable?
- Is it aspirational and inspiring?
- Is it meaningful and not too generic?
- Is it memorable?
- Does it resonate?

Now, have fun finding yours!

Top Tip:

Our recommendation would be to revise the document every twelve months or so, as part of your overall review of the company culture. Does the culture still serve its purpose, does it help you to get to the next level? If not, you can work on them and make changes.

Don't forget to communicate the changes.

Introducing your Cultural Statements

You can visualise and introduce your cultural statements to your team creatively in lots of ways, of course. They shouldn't just sit in an archive on a shared drive somewhere. In fact, if they did that, there wouldn't be much point in having them. Use your main communication channels and make them appealing and prominent like your all hands meeting, a screensaver for all employees, or a banner on your intranet. Furthermore, you could use bags with your logo and vision statement printed on them. Or how about branded water bottles, mobile phone protection, or printed coffee mugs in your kitchen. You can make a huge campaign out of it. Just search online for merchandise and select Images. That's how I always got inspired for my cultural campaigns. But before you get carried away with your creative ideas, a presentation in an all-hands meeting and a follow-up email will do the trick.

Top Tip:

Create memories and momentum with your teams.

How about an extraordinary surprise all-hands meeting, where there is juice/sparkling wine waiting for everyone and a cake in the form of the new logo? You could have vegan cupcakes with your logo as chocolate garnish. And how about a fun facts presentation about how much coffee has been consumed over the last months, how the banana intake has increased in correlation with the development of the cultural statements or your new branding?

It will lift everyone's spirit and keep the culture alive and in everyone's head, if certain cultural milestones are being celebrated, like the introduction of your new branding and new logo, your 100th employee, the introduction of your Vision and Mission statements etc. It can be small and budget-friendly but memorable. Maybe you can find a balloon dealer, where you can order a man-sized '100' made of balloons?

You could print out your cultural statements and actually sign them physically as founders and send them to your early team. Believe us, those little things will be remembered and talked about for years – and so will your culture!

Out of experience, there will always be those few creative and involved people in startups, who happily take up the challenge of organising such an event with/for you. Just give them a budget and ask for veto-rights. You might be surprised about the truly authentic outcome.

1.3 Getting Up and Running

Understanding your Culture

As your company keeps growing and you are adding new members to the team, you want to create a platform that allows for equality and scalability.

As Boryana Straubel (Generation Collection & Straubel Foundation) says:

'Write your company culture down and communicate it regularly. Model the culture for your team, be the role model.

Knowing your culture and communicating it, will help you and everyone else to make decisions on spending, company timelines and objectives and how to create company policies that will affect parts of your business, including interaction between your teams or customers and suppliers for example.'

So, how do you make sure all your employees know, understand and comply with your company culture even beyond the cultural co-founder team, who were involved in the creation of it? How do they know how to behave, what to do, how to collaborate? How do they know what they, as part of the company stand for, what to value and what to push for? How do you keep your culture communication alive?

At Tesla, Lilium and other startups we saw some great practices, we want to share with you now. There are many creative ideas out there and there is no right or wrong. These are just some examples of what you can do, we hope it will get you thinking about what you could use, adapt or reinvent for use in your company. Let's start with how you should continuously communicate your culture, so it keeps being 'a thing' without annoying anyone in the long run.

Wall Displays and Postcards

Have wall posters made up or artwork created that share your values and hang them up in a central spot. Then let every team member sign their names underneath as a sign of commitment. You can have postcards designed and printed with your logo and mission statement. Your team will proudly send them to their friends and family. Or how about posting one, snail mail, to themselves or each other with some added notes about what's important to them?

At Lilium, we sent such a postcard to every new hire with handwritten warm welcome wishes from their respective manager, signed by the respective team.

But keep in mind, how you behave yourself is one of the biggest factors of all. What you DO has far more impact on what you write down than what you WANT people to do. Culture is a living thing. The statements support it – but they don't create it. You do, and your team does. No document can replace the walking example that the founder shows everyone on a daily basis.

Mind the Gap in the Onboarding Process

The process of onboarding new people is something that is often overlooked but the first impression and first three months are the most important for your new hires, so it is important to get right. Not only does it get them up to speed quickly and working productively, but it's also the first opportunity to align new team members to your company's culture and ways of working, right from the start.

At Lilium, every new hire had some meetings pre-scheduled in their calendar for their first two weeks, which were mandatory to join as they allowed them to fully understand the culture. For example, one slot would be at the IT department, where they would receive their gear and could ask questions regarding the process of setting everything up. Another meeting was with the co-founders, who introduced them to the story, the mission, vision and values of Lilium. It gave the founders the chance to welcome people personally and make that important connection. Meggy met with new hires to explain the Employee Referral Program and how we hired with culture in mind, while another colleague of ours in HR had a meet and greet with them to chat about all contractual matters, payroll, health and safety.

Then, the new employees met with Mareike, to guide them through our internal communication tools landscape while I got to share how we work together. During those meetings Mareike received a great deal of positive feedback from new colleagues, who were awestruck about how personal and organised the process was, how the experience made them feel even prouder to be working at Lilium and how welcome they felt from day one. Of course, we tried to automate certain steps and make it more efficient as we scaled up, but we held on to as much of the personal experience as we could. It was the backbone of getting people up and running in *The Way We Do Things Around Here*. We didn't just tell people that we are an inclusive team; by meeting the co-founders, they were part of the team. We didn't just talk culture, we walked it with them.

Team Meetings

How about organising a regular all-hands meeting and bring the whole team together? Maybe call it something different to make it feel special. At Lilium, we called them our All-WINGS Meetings (as we were an aviation startup). Make it a mandatory weekly thing, where everyone has the *privilege* to participate and hear the latest news and updates from every corner of the company, especially from management. Use this meeting to re-energise and re-align your team to the culture.

So How Can You Bring the Big Four to Life?

Story telling

In one startup, one of the co-founders occasionally stopped in the middle of the hallway, in the kitchen, or in the middle of a conversation, making notes in his mobile phone. When he was asked what he was doing, he replied, 'I'm collecting stories'. Whenever he overheard a conversation or witnessed someone doing something that aligned really well with their culture, he took notes, which he then presented in their regular whole team meeting – of course with the permission of the people involved. These little stories were living examples and gave encouragement for how he and his co-founders wanted their culture to be lived. 'Our Culture' was a fixed point on the meeting agenda each week. They made their culture more relatable and understandable. They showed the team, which behaviour and which actions were valued, and which were unwanted. It also showed that people's actions were being noticed and evaluated and that the leaders took the culture seriously. Point out to your team what sets them and your company apart from others. It instils pride and people love to speak about the things they are proud of.

Share and shine

Ask your team to share their stories as well! People feel valued when they are heard. Give them the opportunity to share and shine. You get the added bonus of learning how they interpret your culture and can act if necessary. Maybe introduce recognition awards or give employees a chance to collect 'culture tokens'. Culture tokens are voted for by the team and given to anyone who is seen to be actively partaking in good team work. Let your teams take an active part. Sit back, listen and observe.

Praise and recognition

If someone in the team does something well which demonstrates your values in any way, or achieved something, even if it's just a small thing, then say thank you or well done, even if you don't share it with the whole team. If someone gave you feedback or challenged you on a certain topic which made you change your mind and decide differently or prompted you to take action, where you otherwise wouldn't have, let them know. A little thank you, or well done, goes a long way and automatically reinforces your values.

Unwanted behaviour

As much as you should acknowledge and promote desired behaviour you need to make sure unwanted ones get called out and eventually even sanctioned. Depending on the severity and manner of misbehaviour your range of disapproval goes from a private warning to letting someone go. You will know when and which reaction from your side is required. Most important, however, is that you react and are consistent, transparent, respectful to the employees affected, confidential and fair about it. We'll address this topic again later.

Culture Survey

The Future of Work says there won't be any surveys in the future but it fails to say how employee's happiness, which is the pulse of your company and your culture, will be measured instead. So, we personally still highly recommend that you conduct regular surveys with your whole team – maybe every quarter or half year. Don't overcomplicate things. There are lots of great, very easy, mostly free survey tools which you can use. Simply sit down and develop a short list of core questions. For example "Do you feel your opinion is valued?", "Do you feel you have the opportunity to learn and grow?". Use a fixed five points-scale, which makes the results specific and measurable. When researching for questions and evaluation possibilities for our early pulse surveys, we consulted the free online publications of Management company Gallup.

Our experience tells us that just 5-7 questions are enough. Not too much for it to feel like an inquisition, but enough to give you a feel for what's going on. In later surveys, stick to the same questions so you can compare and see the development over time.

	STRONGLY DISAGREE	DISAGREE	UNDECIDED	AGREE	STRONGLY AGREE
Do you feel your opinion is valued?	○	○	○	○	○
Do you feel you have the opportunity to learn and grow?	○	○	○	○	○
Do you receive meaningful recognition for doing good work?	○	○	○	○	○
Do you have access to everything you need to perform to the best of your ability?	○	○	○	○	○
Do you know what constitutes good performance in your role?	○	○	○	○	○

Once you have collected the answers, save them for later comparison and do something with them! If you can derive any objectives from them, develop a roadmap to improve things for your people. Make a plan and communicate it! Then act upon your plan and communicate that as well!

Your team needs to hear that you took their feedback in that survey seriously, regardless of whether the main points were good or bad, and they need to know what you are going to do about them. This will encourage them to give feedback in general, participate in future surveys and show them that they are being valued and heard and that they have the potential to change things.

Transparency and Honesty

Using great companies as inspiration and role models, or even copying certain aspects from their culture and the ways they do things is a clever thing to do. There's a lot to learn, and why should you invest time and effort in reinventing the wheel, when it's been perfected elsewhere?

Google is not a startup anymore, but they have been known for their great company culture all along. One of Google's core components was, according to Laszlo Bock, the Senior Vice President of People Operations the 'Default to open'. In their weekly meeting, famously called TGIF (Thank God It's Friday), they not only shared information and updates, but established an environment of transparency where everything was up for debate. The two founders Larry Page and Sergey Brin always hosted the meeting personally, which made it a special and valued event. Every employee was encouraged to ask questions beforehand, which could be voted for, and the most voted for were the questions that the team most wanted answered.

Of course, there is confidential information, which insiders can't share with just anyone. That's always the case with internal information sharing. When that's the case, be transparent about that. Tell your team why you cannot share it (yet) and give them the information you can share. They will understand that certain topics are under legal restrictions, are confidential or are simply not ready to be shared yet.

As long as you keep your team updated about where the company is headed and why it's going in a certain direction, people will feel like part of something greater than just their day job.

Companies that value collaboration, the exchange of ideas and encourage transparency will develop a positive atmosphere in the office leading to more productivity, lower staff turnover and better relationships.

So, keep your door – literally – open as often as you can and invite your team again and again to come in and talk to you in person. Agree with your leadership team to do the same. Be approachable.

If you as the founder or CEO don't stand behind your culture, no one will. You need to have a sparkle in your eyes when you talk about your vision. You have to be passionate about your mission. Be a true and authentic ambassador for your culture and make it second nature to live it.

Take Pride in it

Once your pride gets involved, you'll fight tooth and nail [for it]
James Clear
(Author of Atomic Habits and a speaker focussing on habits, decision making, and continuous improvement)

The more pride you have in certain aspects of your company culture, the more motivated you will be to maintain, nurture and develop them further. Taking pride in your culture and your team will make you care for it even more and you will be able to see the results of that, we promise.

We have seen the results of founders and leaders who took

pride in their team and their culture and we can tell you it is an infectious feeling of passion and the desire to be part of it, when you see and hear those leaders speak about it.

Of course, you can be proud of a new funding round secured, a working prototype produced, good press coverage and a new revenue record and so on. All these things can, and should, be celebrated as they are truly great achievements. But truly living up to your culture and having a great team are just as good reasons to be proud and celebrate. Keep that in mind and express it. If you feel proud of your team and how your culture is thriving, share it. If you do feel joyful to be surrounded by loyal and hardworking people, who make your vision come true and who live YOUR culture, then celebrate them!

To celebrate, organise a day off together and go somewhere outdoors where you then go sledging, build igloos, have a picnic with games etc. There are many companies which offer such team events for any team size and budget. Regular off site team building events are a great investment and cannot be underestimated.

Top Tip:

Imagine your culture is a lever which connects and aligns people. Consider these points to make it an authentic one.
• Treat your employees as customers

• Make your on-boarding process memorable and a celebration of a new start for Every! Single! New hire!

• Use every single opportunity to promote and speak about your culture, internally and externally. Make it part of your pitch and authentically live it wherever you go

1.4 When Things Go Right

Personal Growth

❝ *A company thrives when people grow* ❞
Mareike Mutzberg

A startup is a place where almost everything seems free, open and possible. Free to take decisions and act without much bureaucracy, open to anyone, any culture, any idea and possible to have different hats on, to thrive and develop. The last point is one of the most powerful employee incentives you can offer regardless of your company size or status. Even in a more static, bureaucratic and structured company with limits to free expression of mind, lifestyle and ideas, taking care of a real opportunity for training and development is a key element for happy and productive employees. Taking this seriously, shows that you care about the evolution of your team members´ careers, which is a powerful expression of employee appreciation.

Therefore you need to allocate an educational budget to your People department; but the benefits of it, foremost the increase in employee well-being, will be worth the investment in the long run.

But please, don't confuse 'facilitating learning' with 'conducting training', which a lot of companies do as it can harm them more than it benefits according to Kelly Palmer, Chief Learning Officer at LinkedIn.

Conducting training means to train employees in something they need for their jobs. Such training aims at growing your company's profits.

But offering real learning opportunities is about investing in people personally, providing value to them and help them become better in any regard such as learning a new language, stress coping methods or presentation and rhetoric skills. This might also benefit their job directly but that's not the intended purpose. The purpose of offering learning opportunities is to show appreciation, increase well-being and motivation and foster their bond with your company. People tend to want to stay at a company where they feel they have real career opportunities outside of their day-to-day business and where they are seen as human beings – not just workers or resources.

Autonomy

We'd like to share another personal insight. We have witnessed so often how you can build team member satisfaction and loyalty through giving people a level of autonomy.

Autonomy is the perceived freedom of choice. People feel autonomous when they perceive that what they do is of their own volition, and that they can decide on their own actions.

Especially in the early days of a startup, for the majority, it's inevitable that every team member is granted a high level of autonomy by default. It is simply that the rules and structures of the company aren't well defined yet and you don't have the capacity or the resources to manage everyone closely. Nor is there a need as you want to push forward, try out, fail fast, develop and grow, which demands a certain amount of freedom and trust in your people.

This inherent autonomy is a good thing, something that we recommend you establish and nurture actively. You, and the leaders in your company, play a big role here since the way you frame information and situations to your team members can either support their feeling of autonomy or undermine it.

For example, make sure the goals and timelines you ask your team members to meet are developed collaboratively. Give them the feeling that they have a say in their schedules and how they do things rather than being micromanaged. On a practical level, instead of phrasing goals and timelines as a given fact, which you will hold them accountable for, formulate those goals as essential information that they need to agree with to be successful in their job.

Autonomy also comes with the avoidance of pressure and stress. A HBR (Harvard Business Review) report states that:

'Sustained peak performance is a result of people acting because they choose to – not because they feel they have to.'

The fact that such basic things as flexible work hours are at the top of most candidates' list of desirable benefits, indicates how important autonomy is to people.

All for One and One for All

This perfectly describes the human need to feel connected to other people, to be part of a group, and to be recognised and appreciated by the people around them.

You can make use of this psychological trait. Your people won't perform solely to receive rewards, but because they are being intrinsically motivated in an environment of solidarity and unity which those rewards represent.

Of course, it is agreeable to receive a financial bonus for an achievement but believe us when we say, this will be forgotten, or worse, taken for granted and expected regularly which you might not be able to keep up financially yet and which might cause friction in the team. But if the 'Coffee-Addict-Award' and the 'Makes-Everyone-Better-Award' that is the people with the highest consumption of coffee and the one who is always there for others, if these were awarded at your last Summer party these awards will stand proudly on their desks or on a shelf at home and they will have meaning within your 'tribe', and only there, thus fostering the feeling of togetherness.

People need to feel connected to, and cared about, by others. If you help your people derive meaning from what they do and why they do it, where they work and whom they work with, you can increase their happiness, therefore their loyalty rises and overall productivity improves.

Ask around and get people's honest feedback about how they feel in the workplace, what they think about an assigned project or goal. Feelings and opinions cannot be argued with, people feel how they feel! So, simply listen and find out what you can do to maintain and further develop any good feedback and how to improve on bad feedback.

When team members know and share your company's values and vision, they connect their tasks with a bigger purpose, and feel that their own personal values are expressed in the way they spend their workdays. When you have a clearly defined and communicated culture and have hired the right-minded people, with a strong 'cultural fit' this feeling of belonging goes a long way to helping your company succeed.

1.5 Scaling – As You Grow

Diversity, Equality and Inclusion – DEI

> *Stop looking at diversity and inclusion as an affirmative action. It is profitable, it enhances performance. We are doing business across cultures and countries, boundaries of legislations. Let it drive your thinking and performance.*
> Winifred Patricia Johansen

To us, Diversity, Equality and Inclusion in business is vital and we want to take this opportunity to draw your attention to it, since we saw how companies benefitted and even flourished from a truly inclusively lived diversity. DEI should be part of your company's core, it should not be used as a window dressing exercise or as an afterthought.

Heterogeneous teams are more effective when it comes to creative processes, such as problem solving. That is why more and more businesses actively seek to attract international talent. But it's not only geographical diversity. When we speak of diversity, we mean people with different gender, age, race, nationality, sexual orientation, religion, handicaps, etc.

> *Diversity is being invited to the party, inclusion is being asked to dance*
> Verna Myers

2022 research by McKinsey gathered data across fifteen countries, from more than 1,000 large companies. The data suggests that the most culturally and ethnically diverse companies outperformed less diverse ones by as much as 36%. Diverse teams are 87% better at making decisions (People Management). Diverse management teams lead to 19% higher revenue. (BCG)

When you think about Diversity and Inclusion, they are interconnected.

Diversity is about representation or the make-up of an entity. And we are not speaking about 'token' hires to mask Diversity and Inclusion. It's not about being able to say, 'we have a female leader, or an African born VP of Product and a Board Member from the LGBT community.'

So, what do we mean? What can you do? The answer is exactly the opposite. Find ways to make every kind of diversity a natural thing, nothing special. When different gender, age, sexual orientation, religion, culture, handicaps, etc. are not a 'thing' to your team anymore, you are on the right track. Start with taking for granted that every single member of your team is a human being with unique abilities, equal rights, as well as opportunities and responsibilities in your company.

> *Equal treatment does not mean that you cannot offer your help to a woman with a small frame, who is carrying a heavy box. Equal treatment means, that you offer the same to a man.*
> Mareike Mutzberg

Create an environment where truly diverse identities are presented, feel included, heard and accepted. Create room for role models within and outside your company. When it comes to hiring, future employees are more likely to join you if they see a representation of themselves on the board, the leadership team and within the company.

Diversity ensures that your product has influences from various different cultures and perspectives. This is not only important for market adoption, but also for innovation and driving your company towards success and sustainability in the long run through diverse ideas and contributions. It's easy to think short term in growing companies, but don't forget to lift your head up and look into the future as it's imperative to the success of your startup.

Cultural Synergy

Bettina Andresen Guimarães, formerly Director of Communications for Citroën Austria as well as Head of international Communications for Citroën/DS and founder of intercultural coaching told us that *'Nancy Adler established the cultural synergy. You need to be able to work with different people, from different backgrounds to allow diversity of thought, embrace different ideas and ensure everyone goes in one direction. Ensure that leadership integrates everyone and lives D&I at their core.'*

Cultural synergy is the combination and interaction of different cultures, which merge into an environment that is based on the combined strengths, perspectives and skills. This new environment basically forms a culture of its own, which is different from the individual cultures from which it derived.

You want to facilitate cultural synergy within your team, so they not only accept cultural diversity, but embrace and live it by synergising. As a result, your team will create and nurture your, and their, own diverse culture, because they see and acknowledge the benefits of it, even beyond the world of work.

So, what do you have to do to make it happen?

The most important thing is to understand the full scope of what intercultural differences comprise. Intercultural differences are quite a complex field and are not yet common knowledge.

Most people underestimate this topic. But it is a very important one, especially in our globalised world, in which the topics of Diversity, Equality and Inclusion receive more and more recognition – as they should, since in many areas we are still far away from this enriching, free, tolerant world in which people naturally live and work inclusively, diversely and equally.

Unfortunately, this topic would get beyond the scope of this book, but since both of us, Meggy and Mareike, are very passionate about it, we wanted to at least draw your attention to it and hope you are one of those making a difference in this world.

What we can do, though, is give you some tips that you can easily apply, from our experience to show you what you can do.

When it comes to geographical cultures you need to do the following things.

Raise awareness

The simplest way to do this is to address the topic directly using your official communication channels. You can ask your team to share an anecdote or research a story about this topic for the next all hands meeting. You can post short lessons learned, in your newsletter or team channel once a week. You could dedicate a section in your intranet to diversity. No matter what you do, keep this topic alive and your team aware of it. The best way to do that, is to engage your team directly in a social and casual way.

Remove bias

Apart from that, we highly recommend including this topic in your hiring and onboarding process. There's no need to overcomplicate things here. Our experience has shown that is efficient and sufficient enough to say something along the lines of 'We currently have twelve nations in our team.

Gestures, mimics and phrases mean different things in different cultures and there are cultural differences in how people work, give feedback and communicate. Please, keep that in mind. And if you ever feel affronted by someone, approach that person openly about it, so you can eliminate future misunderstandings right from the start. We all have the same goal here and depend on each other. So always assume the best intentions!'

Mind the language

Establish a common language of business, which is being spoken by everyone and encourage native speakers to mediate should there be any potential misunderstandings. Create a policy to always talk and write in the common language, you never know if you need to forward something written to someone, who does not speak your mother tongue. Make it the norm to ask someone to repeat themselves, for clarification or to give an example. Visualise information as much as you can by providing data, pictures, videos etc. and make use of storytelling. Stories, analogies and examples are easier to understand for everyone. Promote and practise an open, direct and honest way of communicating and make it explicit. Explain to your team why you are communicating this way and that you expect the same from everyone. Everyone should feel like an intercultural ambassador, encouraging each other to speak up and mentioning the common culture and intercultural differences frequently.

Allow prep time for non-native speakers, not only during official meetings but even during lunch breaks. Be patient and give them enough time to gather their thoughts or to make a point, don't interrupt or talk over them. Most importantly, don't correct their grammar or expression unless explicitly asked to improve their language skills.

Keep all your communication simple

Assuming your common language in your company is English, then use simple English with short sentences. Avoid unnecessary difficult phrases, quotes and references to anything only a native speaker would understand, and certainly don't do jokes and irony, as the acceptance and understanding of it varies greatly between different cultures. Without any intention of discriminating non-native speakers by comparing them to a child, this tip always helped me with finding the right wording. If you imagine explaining something to a five-year old, then you are communicating in a way every non-native speaker can follow easily.

Avoid stereotypes

Being aware of different cultures very quickly turns into thinking in stereotypes without even realising it or meaning harm. As we will see below, you automatically have to work with some kind of stereotype in order to grasp a culture and its peculiarities. But it is simply wrong to rely on stereotypes to make assumptions about the behaviour of colleagues. Being from Spain or Sweden does not dictate every action a person takes or every decision someone makes. Cultural upbringing influences a person only so much. But there is so much more to an individual's personality and behaviour, like experiences, knowledge gained, and the general environment lived in, that you need to take every person as an autonomous individual. Each team member has a unique way of working, behaving and communicating and has personal interests, wishes and preferences. Their original culture does not dictate this, but rather shapes it.

Organise team building events

There are many low and no budget possibilities you can choose from. You can organise international breakfasts, where every team member brings a speciality from their country, celebrate birthdays in the person's cultural way; introduce inclusive lunch tables, happy hours, movie nights showing international movies, team off-site events, etc. But it is important that you do something in this regard. Create opportunities for casual interactions and encourage everyone to come forward with ideas for social events and to organise them, themselves. This will help the team to interact during their downtime and bond with each other.

Also, before starting into a project with a new team, allow some time to simply get to know each other personally and their culture in a casual way. Share stories about your home and country and talk about your cultural customs, so that your team can identify commonalities and hidden biases.

Set a clear framework

Especially for intercultural teams it is crucial that every team member knows the common goal, the accepted ways of working and the ground rules for collaborating. Establish clear roles and responsibilities for each team member and outline what is expected from everyone. In a nutshell, establish your own culture, which accepts and includes every foreign culture but also sets a clear framework with norms and boundaries valid for everyone. Provide spaces for finding common ground, for example by encouraging your team members to create team channels for personal interests, such as hiking, parenting or classic car lovers and dog sitters, where they can find and connect with like-minded colleagues.

Top Tips:

And then there are those little things that matter:

- **Practice empathy:** Empathy is defined as the ability to understand and share someone else's feelings. If a team feels understood, they are more open and inclined to give you, and each other, feedback and ask for help. Conflicts can be overcome quicker and more effectively that way.

- **Never assume:** Empathy pre-supposes an open mind and a readiness to switch perspectives and see things the way other cultures would. In any awkward situation or whenever something feels 'strange' or 'different', ask yourself if this could be a cultural thing and that you might be biased.

- **Avoid creating artificial barriers:** Do not talk politics unless there is a significant shift in the world where you need to make a statement. The statement should always be factual, with empathy but not emotionally charged. With religion or other controversial issues always remain nonpartisan. Be sensitive about the office decoration, accepted dress code and behaviour. Make them neutral and safe for everyone.

- **Mind the cultural customs:** Proactively accommodate different work schedules. For example, allow siestas, be sensitive of Ramadan rules and so on. Be mindful of each culture's list of holidays. Be sensitive to dietary and religious restrictions in choosing restaurants and selecting food for bigger meetings or celebrations. This shows respect and consideration.

As mentioned before, intercultural diversity is not only geographical. A 24-year-old Swedish woman and a 56-year-old Swedish woman can be considered to have different cultural backgrounds in certain regards. So, we would like to encourage you to go back to the start of this subchapter and read our guidelines again – now with 'gender, age, sexual orientation, handicap, etc.' in your mind, every time you read the word 'culture'.

So here's what you can do when it comes to the personal cultures:

You should also
- **Raise awareness** of LGBTQ issues, the gender pay gap, family friendliness, age related difficulties at the workplace.

- **Mind the language** when talking about age or handicaps etc. Decide which terms are OK to use, what is OK to say about or to ask a handicapped person.

- **Keep all your communication simple** and don't beat around the bush. Say what you want to say in a correct and polite, yet easy to understand and clear way. Also make sure, your work environment and processes are reachable, understandable and usable by everyone, e.g. your manual and training for a new system should speak to everyone within your company, regardless of their years of experience or background.

- **Avoid stereotypes** when it comes to any (minority) group: women, old and young people, people without a higher education, LGBTQ, handicapped people.

- **Organise team building events** also under the motto of equality for all.

- **Set a clear framework** for how to treat each other no matter the sexual orientation, gender, age, religion and so forth.

- **And do all the other little things that matter** for a really inclusive and intercultural corporate culture in every sense of the word.

To sum things up: do bring together a diverse team and take care of a healthy, inclusive diverse environment. As Winifred Patricia Johansen puts it:

'Ensure you have the right people for the right job, retrospectively from everything that comes with their background, preferences etc. Give people a chance. If you exclude people on the basis of their names, or what they look like you lose out on value. [... Differences are] part of the population, if you filter out on certain criteria, you lose value. Look at what people can add. People have a lot of grit and drive when they want to prove something, it makes them high performers. Elevate people, develop people within your organisation who have the ability and willingness to grow.'

Sustainability

> *The greatest threat to our planet is the belief that somebody else will save it.*
> Robert Swan,
> the first man in history to walk to both the North and South Poles.

At Lilium, sustainability is a very important value that drives the company. We always tried hard to find and implement a sustainable solution, partner, or service for everything, from production line to office supplies and even our canteen. We offered 'Lili-bikes' that every team member could use so they could get from one building to another across the Munich campus in a sustainable way. We helped Lilians to organise car sharing to and from work and provided a shuttle bus from the S-Bahn station directly to the Lilium- buildings on airport grounds. We introduced 'Meatless Monday' and always strove for local and organic food. We recycled waste and introduced a paperless office policy.

We cannot say this enough: we personally believe that startups have the opportunity and power to change the world.

The world is an ever changing place. Environmental, economic, and social sustainability is a must in today's business environment. It adds brand value, it ensures and increases a loyal customer base in a world where people start to increasingly make conscious purchasing decisions.

An environmentally aware business considers more than just profits. The company's impact on society and the environment is an important and integral part of the organisation. Businesses that are looking at sustainability, consider the health of the structure within which it operates, helping to construct an environment in which the business can thrive.

There is another side to sustainability in the sense that more and more employees and job seekers want to ensure that the companies they work for share their values.

Candidates will look at your company and make a judgement based on the information they see and hear. If your company has a bad reputation and doesn't act in an economical and socially responsible way then people will be put off. They don't want to work for an employer that is perceived to have no commitment to the environment. It creates a barrier for them as they don't feel that they can talk about the services the companies offer as there is no pride. Often there will be guilt or shame.

Forbes stated in his late 2021 article about retention of staff that Environmental, Social and Governance (ESG) themed investments have become one of the best performing investment categories in recent years, paving the way for continued growth of this strategy.

Consider the above and ask yourself...

1. Do you want to be the one that drives change, or responds to change?

2. Do you want to contribute to the problems we have in this world, or do you want to find alternatives and solve these problems?

3. What do you want to be remembered for?

4. Can you and your teams reduce waste and increase recycling in your company?

5. Can you implement sustainable practices within your supply chain?

6. Can you get your team involved in volunteering activities around ESG?

Your Culture Wrap Up

- **It's beneficial to start creating your culture early and to be intentional about it.** Pick and choose cultural documents wisely and in accordance with your overall business goal, your industry and the nature of your company. In the beginning, it might be sufficient to start with a vision and a mission statement and values.

- **Communicate your culture** and embed in everything you do.

- **Be personally authentic.** Live and communicate the company's values.

- **Simplicity wins.** Don't overcomplicate things in the beginning. Start with some basics but know where you're heading and what you might need later on.

- **Mind the true implications of cultural diversity.** Make it a deeply rooted and sincere way of living in your company and create cultural synergy.

- **Engrain employee experience as part of your culture.** Treat your team like you would treat your customers.

- **Put diversity first,** in all its aspects.

RECRUITING

Learn the art of identifying, attracting, screening and interviewing top talent.

2.1 What and Why

How We Do Recruitment Round Here

' Hiring people is an art, not a science '
Meggy Sailer

Larissa applied for a job at a biotech startup, a company of less than 100 people.

She spent hours in the interview process, met the Founder and Co-Founders for two hours, the VP of Operations for another hour as well as the VP of Product for one and a half hours. Prior to that, she had zoom calls with some of these interviewers as well.

If you count the original conversations with the recruiters, she spent a good six to eight hours within this recruitment process, over the period of two months.

She finally received an offer. Larissa was over the moon, she had met great people, she was told about the amazing working culture and all the exciting projects she would be involved in. She handed in her notice at her current company and two months later, she joined the Biotech startup.

Within the first week she noticed that people weren't very happy. There seemed to be no alignment across the company.

In the second week she noticed that people were leaving within two or three months of joining. Towards the fourth week, she reached out to the interview panel to schedule a follow up meeting in the diary to continue to build on the existing relationship. During a conversation with her manager, she got confused as she was discouraged by her manager to reach out to these people. Instead, her manager informed her about the tasks she had to do to make an immediate impact. They were completely different though from what was discussed during interview. It almost sounded like a different job.

Larissa wanted to give it her all, despite having a strange feeling that things weren't right. She put her head down and got to work. Three months later and she had still not seen the founders in person, there was no direction on the company's goals, vision or mission and she noticed that people weren't working in parallel. The teams didn't function well, team members were working on their own on tasks, which were dished out daily.

For more than six months she continued to attempt to influence the founders and leadership team when she finally got hold of them. She suggested implementing certain changes, but it fell on deaf ears. She felt like she was working in a larger organisation with silos, which isn't what she wanted at all. Most importantly she could not understand why the company was so different from what she experienced during the interview process.

More people joined and left within months, the company had a 45% turnover rate and it was chaos. Eventually Larissa was approached by another firm, left and never looked back. When people asked her about the biotech startup, she didn't have much good to say about the company as you can imagine.

The essence of the story is clear.

Within the first six months an employee comes out of their initial learning phase and becomes effective. As a company, you are paying the price for spending time and resources during the recruitment, onboard & training phase and then have people leave.

High turnover raises eyebrows internally and externally. Your investors and board members will most likely put you under a magnifying glass. A high staff turnover could hinder everyone's ability to succeed in business.

You are never 'just' hiring people; in hiring, you are sowing seeds for your company to thrive. And that takes time and effort before you can actually 'harvest' the wider benefits.

Recruitment as Differentiator

Recruitment is often treated like a band aid. People are hired to solve immediate growing pains that a company is experiencing without a real thought around the longer term vision.

Companies that get it right have a business plan that is at least 12-18 months out. Or ideally twenty-four months if you dare and want to level up. As a business they understand what they need in order to achieve their business goals and how the right hires, at the right time will enable them to get there. Don't get us wrong, from time to time you may need to react to unforeseen circumstances by taking people on to fill sudden gaps. You may have recently won a large project and need to hire people quickly. That's OK. Hiring this way should not become the norm, however, as it leaves you wide open to vulnerabilities within your company.

When you have a goal driven plan that's adjustable and a little flexible in terms of how you get to your overall goal, you will be much more successful. The same applies to your life, when you set goals, you are more focussed.

Once you have understood the power of seeing the people and recruitment function as a strategic arm of your overall business, you have levelled up to successfully scaling your company.

Prof. Claas Triebel (Perform Plus & Growth Academy), who gave us his time during the production of this book, put it very nicely. *'Think of your startup as a premature baby, which still needs to develop even the most essential features to live. You would only let the most important people near your baby, those who will nurture and care for its most essential needs to survive and who can bear that responsibility.'*

We are here to share our experience with you to set you up for success and there is a good reason for it.

Looking at the bigger picture, research shows that 90% of

startups across Europe and the US, fail within their first three years.

<hr>

Top three reasons for startup failure:

1. No real market need for the product
2. Ran out of cash
3. Not hiring the right team

If the failure to hire a stellar team is the third reason why startups end up failing, why aren't more founders/founding teams paying more attention to it? Because they are ignorant.

Boryana Straubel (Generation Collection & Straubel Foundation) told us that she firmly believes that people are your currency. *'Why wouldn't a founder invest in exceptional people and create a solid culture from day one?'*

Winifred Patricia Johansen (Senior vice-president for commercial affairs for Quantafuel ASA, Chair of the Board of Quantafuel Skive ApS, Denmark) shared research with us that shows clear evidence that companies with great, diverse teams are more successful. *'I have been saying the same thing to founders for the last twenty years; the value of the company equals the quality of the talent,'* she told us. She's right.

You will build a more employee centric organisation when you understand that people are your most important asset.

After all, no company is just the founder, and if it is, you don't have a company – you have merely created a job for yourself!

Customers often want to know how companies treat their workforce, they want to know that their money is invested well and that they are supporting something they can believe in. Your people are the fundamental component. When they have the right mindset, they are more likely to tell everyone they meet about the purpose of your company. Your people will be your greatest advocates and evangelists. If your company becomes known as a great place to work, it's a destination point and a great selling point for your product or service.

Top Tip

When you think about recruitment, always think about what you need for your company to succeed, not just want you want or is nice to have.

What we mean by that is, be strategic. Maybe there is this one A-hire you would like to have in order to make a public announcement and get some media coverage after your seed round. But think ahead and ask yourself if that will really drive business forward. This person is probably expensive and at this stage you are better off spending that money on people who can actually develop, build and sell your product and service to create a more solid proof of concept.

Unicorns Do Exist

Do you have the ambition to become a unicorn? If so, there is nothing wrong with that! Or is this the first time you have heard about them in a corporate context?

Well, those still rarely spotted unicorns, which are privately held companies with a value of over $1 billion do exist. Even though only a handful of companies ever get to these valuations, we want to encourage you to dare to dream.

There has never been a better time to create a company. The

funds are certainly available. With global interest rates at an all-time low, the world is awash with money that is looking for a good return on investment.

There are whole industries re-shaping how they work with the use of AI and with the world as it is today sustainability is an increasingly important focus. Healthcare and personal care industries are becoming more accessible to all and going digital. Some Industries hadn't changed much for a long time until now; for example the energy and the transport sectors. These sectors are wide open for innovation. They have previously been pioneering industries and there's more opportunity now, more access to cash, more access to talented people with fewer geographical boundaries, who can work for you, than in the history of man. It's a time for huge optimism and a time to dream big, think big and have bold goals.

Even if you don't have the ambition to become a unicorn, or you don't have it at the moment, we know that inspiring and driving ambition amongst your team in a startup plays a vital role.

If you have being a unicorn in your sights, how would you get there? And if you don't, what can you learn from them that will help you to achieve your measure of success?

Well, first of all, it's worth a mention that both of your authors have experience of being part of not just one, but two unicorns; Tesla and Lilium.

Unicorns tend to be disruptors and often have a first mover advantage. Often, they are first to go to market. They have an eye on expanding their product and service and continue to innovate.

According to a study from i5invest and i5growth, as of February 2022, there are more than 1,000+ unicorns around the world. Europe has 123 of them. To name a few; SpaceX, Google, Lilium, Gymshark, Impossible Foods, Masterclass, MessageBird, Bitpanda, Udemy, Fair, Clubhouse, Klarna, Rivian, Northvolt, Hopin, Graphcore, Calendly.

The stories behind these companies are incredible and we have a lot to learn from them. We are seeing a trend that unicorns are no longer specific to the US. Europe is a major player and that fact is here to stay.

Consider the story of Lilium. The company was founded in 2015 by four engineers and PhD students from the Technical University in Munich. Daniel Wiegand, the CEO and Founder, believed that it was time for a change. He wanted to push the boundaries of physics. When he set out to create his team, the focus and ambition was to build a prototype and eventually expand into mass market to create a product that enables a world where anyone can fly anywhere and anytime.

The team always has, and still does, think big. The goal is to revolutionise the world of personal transport. In the early days, the founders were always open to possibilities and flexible in their approach on how to get there. Their purpose, drive and vision had them always focussed forwards. They set off to create a stellar team. With that in mind, they expanded and strategically surrounded themselves with some great investors, teams and board members. In 2020 Lilium received its unicorn status. By September 2021 the company went ahead with its IPO at Nasdaq through a SPAC deal with Qell.

Hard work pays off when you work towards your dreams.

Building a Team of Winners

There really is no substitute for the people you surround yourself with.

You can have the best vision, mission and culture, but it's all meaningless if you don't have an engaged team that works together, is fulfilled, driven, relentless and passionate. It's the people within your team that will enhance your original idea for your company. And it's them, together with you as a founder, who will bring the product or service to life and into this world.

It's not just about building a team of winners, it's about leading them and creating a space that allows everyone to pivot, thrive and be successful.

Meggy shares with us some of her personal experience.

Meggy's Story

When I joined Tesla, famous for its R&D, they had recently produced the first Roadster and they were gearing up for the Model S, with more products in the development stage. There was a real ambition from the founding team and the people surrounding them to grow the company and take the world by storm.

At Tesla we were on the lookout for people from all walks of life who were at different stages in their life who could bring their experience to solve problems, who were willing to go the extra mile and work hard. These people were talented, able to work in teams, willing to take risks, make mistakes, focus and learn from them and make things better.

Elon's, and the founding teams' vision was always strong and intentional. And it was clearly communicated through the whole company, with conviction and a lot of energy. We all knew that we worked together towards a common goal; a goal that was greater than us.

Everyone who joined Tesla at the very early stages knew that we were up against an existing industry, not to mention the strong lobby of car manufacturers all over the world, and it would be hard.

And by goodness, it was.

How we recruited was very different from any other company that I had ever worked in and it completely resonated with me. We always looked for specific traits in people as mentioned. It wasn't just about their work history and if they could do the job which is how so many other companies hired at the time. At Tesla it was more about their mindset, their ability, drive and motivation. Of course, experience was a decision point too, but it was never the first thing we looked at like other companies do.

We hired people who were as focussed as the founders to make Tesla successful, at any cost. And the hard work paid off, and it still does.

The Road to success is long, but when you win, it is victorious.

Most early startups suffer from the same challenges. They are strapped for cash, and often feel that they cannot attract the right talent. If you feel like this right now, rest assured that you are not alone.

When startups get their first fundamental cash injection funding round (Seed or Series A) they often still struggle to attract A players. People who have experience and worked for companies that you admire and add strategic value to your company aren't easy to attract in general.

If you feel you just can't get the people you want, here are some things that you can do.

Your company culture is a key differentiator, and we said it already: it's a tool to attract and retain talent. Use it through the whole recruitment, onboarding process and your employees' lifecycles. Base your employee experience on it. Make sure you have nailed this down and that you are open to evolving it.

Don't underestimate the power you hold as a founder within the recruitment process. People will buy into you as much as the rest of the interview team and the job you offer.

Use your recruitment process as a pitching ground, without giving away sensitive company information or IP. Share the market opportunity. Allow candidates to get a glimpse of where they can bring their experience and help your company to get to the next level. Paint a vivid picture of the company's mission and how they can learn with you to drive things forward.

Top Tips:

- If you want to attract that A player, ensure that the candidate gets an understanding of the calibre of people who sit on the board, or are advisors to your company and those who invest in it and their vision for the company on top of what we just shared.

- Use your network and get buy-in on your A-players in strategic positions from investors or board members. Let them speak to the finalist candidates to ask questions and share their vision of your company and vice versa.

- You managed to attract some A players. Make the most of it and communicate this internally and externally. Use your channels, send out a press release to show the outside world that you mean business and it will help you to attract other people.

- Inspire people around you with these press releases and show them that you mean business. If you have investors, let them know first before you go external. You can do this within very close timelines. On the same day as the person starts. Shout it out to the world via the media on the day the person starts with you and what they will be doing at your company and leverage the feedback. Have a plan for which type of media and which channels should be used. Choose those that are strategically useful for your company.

2.2 – How to Set It up

Hiring

As a founder, it may be that you think 'I'm creating something new here, new jobs, new possibilities, a new culture that people will love and stay here for good', and that's it. In some cases may is be true, but in practise it's not quite like that. Working with your people requires you and your leadership team's ability to adapt over time and make changes as you go along.

Employees will inevitably come and go, depending on how you interact with them. But there are things you can always do to create a good structure to minimise the impact of turnover by creating a solid employee experience.

Employees are typically looking for a decent living wage, growth opportunities and a place where they can learn and grow. And if we go back to purpose and culture, they are looking for their basic human needs to be covered such as security as well as the feeling of being accepted and heard.

Building stellar teams is important. Assembling and working with the right founding team is, however, crucial.

Founding partners and early teams form in various ways from meeting people through education, friendship, at events or through their spouses. Some will meet their co-founders at University. It starts as early as writing a dissertation that involves building a company or having an idea and inviting a bunch of people to join you in a room to start a business, like Mark Zuckerberg did at Facebook. The founders of Microsoft, Bill

Gates and Paul Allen met at school and teamed up again later in life. Jerry Yang and David Filo were two Stanford Graduates who decided to found Yahoo together back in 1995.

Airbnb co-founder Nathan Blecharczyk moved to San Francisco and found a roommate through Craigslist, Joe Gebbia. At the time, Blecharczyk was an engineer for a startup and Gebbia was a designer for another startup and they immediately hit it off. After Blecharczyk moved out, Gebbia's college friend Brian Chesky moved in. All three became close friends and worked in the same industry and it was in the summer of 2008 when they came up with their billion-dollar idea.

Now these are all stories of people who made it but remember that 90% of startups don't make it; they don't have a real plan, a place in the market or the right team.

It's a privilege to be a leader and take people on a journey, and so finding the right people to be beside you really makes a difference.

Arnnon Geshuri shared with us his experience on what seems to make the **difference in the success of startups when it comes to their team, founders and the culture.** He told us:

'When you hire and encourage passionate people, let their passion guide them to make the company better. It's important to remember that great people attract more great people. If you have superstars, they know more superstars. Make sure these people are on your hiring panel, it will be inspirational for candidates and help recruit them.

Candidates want to work with amazing people who make them better – so who you put on your interview panel is critically important to showcase your company. If you crack these things, you are ahead of the game.

Link the purpose of your company to their day-to-day work. Make sure your team understands how their role is connected to the company and overall goal, ensure they understand the higher purpose. This will help inspire them to do better and go above and beyond in their role and help others on the team be successful'.

When you create a company and you don't pay attention to people or culture you can end up with a lot of confusion and even despair between people. Nobody means for things to go wrong, they just have a habit of going wrong when people are working in a cultural vacuum. That's because each person will do what they think is right and important, but it may not align with your overall goals or with the other people in the team. The culture, that idea of *The Way We Do Things Around Here*, helps folks to make the right decisions, and make those right decisions to travel in the right direction.

If you have open and fluid communication, it will drive innovation and connectivity. We have seen companies succeed that encourage debate with opposing opinions voiced which celebrate differences and create courageous conversations. Don't just hire people to say yes to everything you want, get people who professionally challenge you. It will make your product and company better.

Founders have split up when they weren't aligned as people, in their mission or in the company culture. You want to spend time building your company, not arguing over little details and strategy. That's not just a waste of time, but a massive waste of emotion and energy too.

This is a good time to share some of the interviews we had with our experts around what makes founders and their teams successful.

The excitement of founding a company is big, positive and full of possibilities.

There is a reason why we want you to pay attention to your co-founder(s).

What we have seen over the years, in public, in private, or every day when things go wrong between founders, is real.

Teams of founders who don't agree with each other in every way during everyday life is perfectly normal, but it must be done behind closed doors! If you display your disagreements out in the open, it can, and probably will, unbalance the whole company.

If the **founding team** does not speak favourably of each other publicly it can create distrust. If founding teams go so far as belittling others, blaming or fighting in front of staff, in meetings or in the office, it often instils similar behaviour in the teams. It does happen and you end up with a team that doesn't trust each other and doesn't work well together.

As a result, your team will be less productive quicker than you think, they'll be focussed on office politics and, even worse, are likely to mirror your behaviour. Not to mention the negative atmosphere it creates, which scares away your people.

Make sure it doesn't happen to you!

Think about founding teams where one party has a different level of integrity to yourself. Examples could be someone who thinks that it is OK to make a pass at employees at work. If that happened, do you think that person might overlook sexual harassment cases within the company?

Now don't get us wrong, where there are people, there are feelings, and these things may happen. But if you don't understand how your co-founder sees the world, and you fail to address this, you could end up with a scandal on your hands. These days, these things have a habit of being played out in the media, or social media, and you would have to remove someone quicker than you realise. But by then, a lot of damage might have already been done.

Imagine if one of your founding team members didn't pay as much attention to finances as you do, doesn't believe in clear communication with you or the team when it comes to the financial state of the company. We all have different attitudes to money, so it's easy to see how that could happen. If it did, you would soon have a moral dilemma, because you are now potentially sucked into a situation you never thought you would see yourself in. Let's face it, financing your company is as important as your financial year end statement and tax returns. If your co-founder is trying to hide this from you and you are trusting them, this will eventually be beyond your control. External auditors, tax offices and accreditors will show up and take over. And think about how this will affect your teams and their families, not to forget your credibility and your reputation.

Remember the part of integrity?

What if one of your co-founders thinks it is perfectly fine to use company finances for their private gain or that it is there to solve their personal problems and you only find out through looking through your monthly company finances. Worse if others find out and your whole team gets unsettled and leaves you as quickly as they started working with you.

What if that co-founder believes that they only work on high level things, and never get their hands dirty. What if it turns out that your co-founder does not want to do some of the work that they should be doing but you are not in a position to add another founder. That's a problem, especially in the beginning when you all have to wear lots of different hats; you are all in this together and you will all have to work hard.

Sometimes founders forget that the money given to them from family, friends, business angels, or venture capitalists has people sitting behind it with their own values, beliefs and level of integrity. If you do something that doesn't align with their view of the world, if you don't communicate with them regularly, and keep them up to date with what's happening in your company you may end up with a problem. Either they will not re-invest, or like we said before they will take action or ask you to do so.

Everything you do in business is connected and evolves around people.

'In my journey of helping founders, I came across a startup who had 80% attrition. Nearly as many people left per week as were being hired.

The company asked me to assess the organisation and its culture. Within a couple weeks of interviews and digging into the teams, I found the company was struggling with two factors; creating a learning culture and making sure everyone felt connected. So, we rapidly built a roadmap that ensured people felt connected from day one and the company went above and beyond setting up a great onboarding process, connected people to vision and mission, and clearly explained what to expect and how their work made a difference and linked to the overall goals of the company.

They created training programmes vertically to help grow everyone professionally and horizontally to drive personal growth and self-help. After three months, attrition went down to 17% and stayed there. That's a huge improvement that over time will probably keep the company in business long enough to get the success they are aiming for. With the previous levels of staff turnover, the bad feeling in the office, the huge cost of recruitment and the time lost constantly getting new people up to speed, it's unlikely that they would have pulled through.

Find people that pull the magic out of you.'

We have worked with many company founders and we consider ourselves lucky to have numerous friends who have founded their own companies. When it comes to choosing co-founders, we have heard and seen incredible success stories but we have also heard the horror stories – and they do exist.

We've known of people who founded companies and ended up falling out so badly that they never speak to each other again; or we've known others who set up with another person only to find out later that they weren't really that enthusiastic about the idea and then pulling out at the worst possible moment. We know those who have discovered that their co-founder had even done something illegal.

Keep this in the front of your mind when it comes to making decisions on the people with whom you might set up a company. Do your best to dig deep enough to know what you are getting into so you can make the best decision. Get practical, consider checking their previous involvement in other companies, their history as a director and maybe even a credit check. After all, if this person was to join you on the board, you can be sure that anyone going to lend the company money will do all of these things. You do not want to find out at a later stage that their history either, career or financial, will prevent you from getting bank funding, credit lines or external investment.

Finding your Match

Now let's get back to the big, positive and full of possibilities attitude that we have when a company is founded.

One could argue that finding the right partner to run a business with has the same priority and significant importance as finding the right partner for your life. After all, you spend more time at work during the week, than you do with your spouse.

Our conversations with Dr Georg Wolfgang, (Culturizer GmbH) and Prof. Claas Triebel, the Founder of Performplus, Co-Founder of the Growth Academy as well as Co-Founder and CEO of Skimio, have some useful insights. Triebel is passionate about people and he has dedicated his life to startups and academia.

We wanted to share their wisdom with you.

Dr Georg Wolfgang (Culturizer GmbH, emphasised in our conversation that: *'a central element of success is a strong founding team. They must fit. A founder should bring many of the following traits such as the ability to let go, to delegate, trust, be fair, be transparent and work entrepreneurially.'*

The key questions to ask oneself as a founder is: What does success mean for me? How do I deal with pressure and stress? How do I carry it into the team? Should it be transparent and open or do I want to be a strong leader? How can I show confidence, be the tower of strength I need to be?

We think that the competency model created by our contributor Prof. Claas Triebel (Perform Plus & Growth Academy) is a really useful tool. He shared with us their findings on 'The six key competencies of founders'. As you read through them, feel free to make some notes on where you think you have opportunities to grow, or weaknesses that you think a co-founder could balance out to make the company stronger. Here's Triebel's six key competencies.

1. **Ambiguity:** Has to be able to tolerate insecurities

2. **Proactivity:** Ability to pivot, solve problems and prioritise

3. **Creativity:** Willingness to try new things and make things different

4. **Tolerance for Errors:** Ability to accept that mistakes happen and deal with them constructively and logically

5. **Social competency:** Communication skills, ability to drive and foster communication and collaboration

6. **Resilience:** Ability to prevent and deal with stressful situations.

Practise makes perfect, right?

If you know yourself, and if you can be honest with yourself, you are in a good place to start finding and building a superb founding team that will go through thick and thin, good and bad, and the highs and lows with you. They will add to your set of skills and fill the knowledge gaps, which naturally exist, since no one is perfect – except for a well-fitting team willing to keep practising and improving.

Allow yourself some time to reflect on yourself.

Ask yourself:

1. What are your key personal strengths or areas you want to improve and weaknesses?
2. What are your professional strengths, improvement areas and weaknesses?
3. What are your educational strengths and weaknesses?
4. What areas need attention, and what can you do to initiate change?

It makes sense to answer these questions yourself then ask people close to you to see if your reflections match up with the perception that others have of you. You may be surprised how others may see strengths in you, that you cannot see. The same goes for weaknesses, of course, and you must be honest with yourself.

How to Find a Co-Founder

You may find yourself in a position where you have to look for a co-founder whilst you build your company in your seed stage, or series A stage. Or you may need to replace a founding team member whilst you expand your company.

Often investors will look for companies with a minimum of two founders to ensure the sustainability and longevity of the startup. As much as your unique idea and solid business plan are essential, there are other important factors such as the ability of founders to be self-aware, to have a growth mindset to be willing to learn and adapt themselves and their business and have passion and confidence amongst other things. (See Triebel's list of founder key traits).

There are a few options on how to find a co-founder, if you don't already have someone in mind. You could ask your network, join accelerator programmes with organisations such as Techstars, Founders Institute, Antler, Rockstart, Entrepreneur first, Birdhouse, Microsoft accelerator, Google for startups, Next stars, AngelPad, Y Combinator, 406 Labs, Women's startup Lab, DigitalHealth, FemaleFounders, to name a view across Europe and the US. There are a variety of them. Check out the ones in your local area.

Write a job description, post it at specific universities or advertise the opportunity on external online platforms for example like LinkedIn, Work In Startups, AngelList, or F6s.

Just to be clear, we are not asking you to speak with candidates who only fit your job description 100%. It's as important to look at their ability, attitude, drive and motivation to succeed. But taking the time to reflect what your business needs to be successful is essential. And you will meet great people during any interview process whom you may just end up hiring at a later stage or for a different position.

When it comes to meeting potential talent, we recommend you meet people lots of times in different settings. People can be at their best during one interview, but if you meet them at different times of the day, over a period of time, it will be easier for you to see if there is a consistency in their behaviour. And since this is a special casting – your one and only co-founder role – you can go so far as meeting them casually for a dinner or walk in the park and really get to know each other, which you most likely would not do with any other candidate.

There are a number of things for you to look out for and ask your potential co-founder.

WHAT YOU NEED TO KNOW.
How will your co-founder add to your business?

Ensure that you and your founding team have different operational skills.

If you, for example, have a background that is in business and finance, you might need a co-founder who has a product background such as engineering or software engineering, who will do the R&D part of the business, especially if it's not your expertise.

Or if you are the technical guru, but sales really isn't something you can get to grips with, then look for somebody who has an economics background and understands sales, marketing and how to influence people in a different way.

The more time you allow yourself to think about this, the better.

When you are searching for your co-founder try and look for somebody who could ideally lead the company with you for at least five years.

And with that in mind, you will have different points to consider. Potentially you could look at getting this person on-board part time first, before you both go all in.

You may need to think about making money for yourself within six months or maybe in two or three years. Or, you may actually need somebody who can inject cash in the business as co-founder. All of these are good points to consider and will help you to build a picture of what you need.

HOW TO IMPLEMENT:
After you have had time to think about the initial setup, as we said, it's time to write a job description just as you would for

any other position. This allows you to continuously review your thoughts and help you with your decision in the end. And who knows maybe after meeting several people, you may change some of the things you already noted down, or you may end up with a couple of co-founders.

WHAT YOU NEED TO KNOW.

Does this person get your business idea, and are they as passionate as you are?

Ensure that you find somebody who is into your business idea as much as you are and will bring their own personal take on things.

Does the other person have a solid level of emotional intelligence and energy?

Can you see yourself working with this person when things get hard? How will they respond to you, your teams and customers when it gets stressful? What type of leadership attributes do you want to see in your company?

Do you look at the world differently when it comes to honesty and integrity, work style and how to run a business?

When it comes to honesty and integrity will this person be trustworthy, genuine, and reliable and value other peoples' time and effort?

To further help yourself, build your interview questions around the above and cover topics such as:

HOW TO IMPLEMENT: ASK...
- What excites you about the company/product/services?
- What type of opportunities do you see for us in the market?
- What are your thoughts about, vision of my company, product and business model?
- Do you believe that the business model should or could be

done differently?

- What have you done in your professional life so far that will allow you to perform in this role?
- What is your work style like? At what time of the day or when do you perform your best work?
- Will you need any external resources to help you perform in this role and why? How would you build the team/product/service?
- How do you want us to communicate with each other during positive and challenging times?
- At what point would you be happy to take a step back as a co-founder from the usual day to day?
- Do you have a role model when it comes to leadership?
- What sort of leadership style do you have, or would you like to have, and why are those attributes important to you?
- What sort of leadership style would be unacceptable to you, and why?
- Do you think that leadership and communication style go hand in hand?
- What sort of values do you think we should instil into the company, leadership and overall teams?
- What values are important to you in life and business, and why?
- How do you manage your energy during busy times?
- What do you like to do in your downtime to recharge?
- Can you give me an example of a time where you had to be honest about something that was really hard for you, and/or the other person?
- How does integrity show up in your daily and personal life?
- How do you think communication should be done in any business? Why is that important?
- What do you do when communication breaks down between teams/people?
- What do you need from me as Founder and CEO to be fully effective?

The Candidate Experience

As a startup you are competing in an existing candidate pool, and on top of that, you need to find people who are willing, able and excited to take a risk and join an early funded company. The competition is fierce. You may already have experienced this, and if not you may be about to.

Employer branding done well allows people from outside to get a glimpse of what it's like on the inside of your company. It either can really inspire people, or put them off from applying for a job.

96% of employees agree that alignment of personal values with a company's culture is a key factor in their satisfaction working there. 40% of the Generation Z (18-24) are looking for good training from their employer. 39% of Millennials (25-34) seek career progression opportunities. 55% of Generation X (35-54) find a good work-life balance a very important pull factor towards an employer.[1]

Often employer branding and your culture form organically when you are around 5-30 people. It will be an accumulation of the people you have hired and how you work together every day and what they say about work during their free time. When you think about growth, however, your employer branding should be treated as deliberately as your culture. Then you can ensure that you have the ability to create a great place to work and that you have future-proofed your company so that it can adjust and grow.

Employer Branding starts within the company, it begins with your actions as a founder and the leadership team, and it is about every interaction your team members experience every day.

When your team members go home at night and speak to their spouses, when they meet with friends or meet new people and talk about their job, that is employer branding.

Employer Branding and candidate experience go hand in hand.

It's all part of the bigger picture when it comes to employee experience.

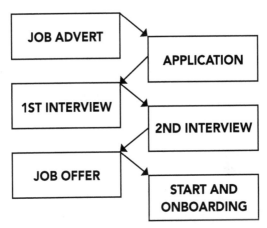

Your candidates are either actively looking for a job, or they may be passive at the moment. They may not be looking for a job, but they may be contacted by your employees out of the blue. It's about the experience they have with your team and potentially yourself during these stages.

How you set the tone from the initial contact, to them becoming an employee and eventually leaving your company, in other words, right through the whole lifecycle of a candidate, is all related to employer branding and the employee's experience.

There is something really powerful in knowing that that the candidate experience you create, can turn things into a real advantage for your company.

A good interview process will help you with your employer branding and allow you to build a reputation in the market, which you may not have at this moment. In many cases it can help you get your company's name and brand out there as people speak to their network about companies they have interviewed with, and the experience that they had.

And of course, in every interview, there is always something in there for you.

Some candidates may become your future customers.

Some candidates may become team members in the future.

You also get a feel for, and understanding of, what type of people are out there and what's happening in your market.

A good candidate experience is important. Who doesn't love to be praised on social media and places like Glassdoor, Fishbowl or Kununu and read positive feedback about their company and interview experience.

We all do!

Now, let's be realistic, haters will always hate and you can try your best to create the very best candidate experience and even then, some people will still not like what you do, especially if the interview feedback they receive hasn't been as positive as they hoped. Some will take to social media to speak about their experience, how they experienced it. And you cannot stop that.

But what you can do is to set yourself up with a process that allows for efficiency, connection in-between your teams, fairness and scalability over time.

Preparation

Consider the Process from the candidate's side for a minute.

———————————— **Tanja's story** ————————————

Tanja applied for a position via LinkedIn with one of LinkedIn's Top 10 tech startups in Germany. As soon as she heard that she was invited for an interview, nervous excitement kicked in. She prepared, did her research and put together questions for the panel.

On the day, she had a terrible commute. It was raining, she missed the bus, the train was delayed and she ended up travelling for three and a half hours. When she arrived at the office in Berlin and was greeted at reception, she was dripping wet and could see a puddle forming on the floor from her umbrella. But Tanja was finally there which made her felt better. She took her chance to freshen up because the interviewer was five minutes delayed herself. She felt like she could breathe again. After ten minutes of waiting she got nervous and after fifteen minutes of sitting in reception past the interview time, she asked the receptionist when the interview would start.

Twenty-five minutes later the head of Product Development showed up and took Tanja into a meeting room. They walked through a few offices and corridors without much interaction. When Tanja sat down it was thirty minutes in and she started to panic, not just because two people entered the room and she had no idea who they were, but she was also concerned about her train back and when she needed to leave to catch it. Eventually one person introduced himself and then the other person from a different department spoke with her while the Head of Product started to read Tanja's CV.

It was forty-five minutes later when the interview really started and Tanja's feeling wasn't improving. The meeting room was small, warm and had a sweaty smell. She wasn't offered another drink, but she was still cold and wet from her terrible journey. The interview was full on, with no space to breathe. After an hour, Tanja had to remind the team that she had to catch a train back home. Some questions were asked that were relevant to the job, but many others were not. In fact, she was asked which spirit animal she had, which was a question she couldn't get her head around at *all. 'What was the relevance of that?' she asked herself.*

When she left, she left with a completely different view of the company compared to what she had expected from the preview and impression given on LinkedIn. She wasn't even able to ask questions because there was no time. People around the office seemed happy and busy, but the interview didn't correlate with her view of what it would be like to go and see this company.

She did receive an offer though, so she asked for an opportunity to speak with other team members to get more info about the company and culture. But that didn't happen. So, in the end, she didn't take the position.

Moral of the story: Don't rest on your laurels just because you have a good reputation, keep working on it, together with your team.

Top Tips:

- Get inspired. Look at brands you admire, what do they do well in your eyes? What could you incorporate in your employer branding?

- Map out the interview process as a team on a whiteboard, use sticky notes or whatever tool works best for you and ask yourself, what would you like people to say about your company's interview process and work out how you can get there. Please see example on page 257.

- Be deliberate and identify the channels you need to use for employer branding from your company website, to LinkedIn, Glassdoor maybe Twitter and Facebook. Create consistency across these channels.

When you look at ever growing organisations such as Apple, Airbnb, Google, Facebook, Microsoft, Tesla, or Amazon for example, recruitment is something that is constant and it's part of the culture of the company as it always has been. The recruitment process and their employer brand has constantly evolved. Pay attention to it and allow yourself and your teams to do the same.

What you should do:

- **Review your employer** branding content regularly on your website, social media, job descriptions and advertisement, every six months initially. Add information as your company grows.
- **Work as a team.** Recruitment is everyone's job. Every individual in your team is an ambassador for your company culture and they probably all know good people, so get your teams involved.
- **Invest in a good Applicant Tracking System (ATS)** like Bamboo HR, or Greenhouse for example. Showcase your culture, departments and open jobs. Make the interaction easy and seamless for candidates.
- **Keep an open mind** when you interview for your existing roles as you may end up hiring some of the candidates you speak with 6-12 months later.
- **Build your brand and gain brand recognition** and people will find you.

Remember that Employer Branding unfolds before and during the actual interview process, continues through the offer / contract stage and you should step things up during the duration of your employees' employment. When you build a solid employee experience your employer marketing will happen automatically. Create a magical employee experience and you will set yourself apart from other companies.

2.3 – Getting Up and Running

Strategy as a Foundation

Arnnon Geshuri, the CHRO of Teladoc Health/Ex Tesla & Google, mentioned that founders or founding teams often struggle with recruitment if they haven't hired before.

'If you don't focus on the culture, you may hire people who might even somehow get things done, but they don't really fit into your company overall. You will find that eventually you will need to part ways with these people, which is a shame and a difficult thing to do because they ARE pushing for it and putting a lot of effort into their jobs. It is just not what your company culture needs. Founders often struggle with difficult team decisions like this, in the early days.

Recruiting correctly, starts with the founding team.

It is important to know yourself. What are you good at? Where do you need to supplement? Which skills are you really good at? What is your background? Be honest with yourself, be true to yourself. This will help you make a strong selection for your founding team and key hires for your company.

Most founders spend time interviewing every single person until the company has about 50-100 people. If people are one of your most important, successful drivers to business, why don't you and your founding team get involved with final interviews for the first 300-600 hires or even your first thousand? Elon Musk does just that. And we know of others as well, so there are no excuses except maybe poor time management and lack of prioritization. It could be simply a thirty-minute call, or getting your interview team together and reviewing their feedback.

As a founder it's an advantage to interview lots of people,

to learn about a particular role or industry and understand the different types of people out there, to make the best possible hiring decisions, at any given time. You will meet people whom you may not recruit in the first six months, but you may recruit them one or two years later when they are a perfect fit.

As your company evolves so you will need different people with various backgrounds and abilities. But the core of the type of person you hire should be in line and should add to your company culture and leadership style.

The internet is full of resources, if you need them, from hiring plan templates to workforce planning tools, or use a simple excel sheet, but as mentioned previously, sit with your core team such as Sales and Product and have somebody in your meeting who looks after finance and understands how to build business plans.

Top Tip:

Ask yourself these questions:
- What are your company goals for next year? Will you be increasing sales by 100% from last year, building an App or building a customer service team? Build a people plan to understand the cost.

- Are you targeting to do business in the Netherlands, Switzerland, the UK or other parts of the globe and if so, why is that important? What will it cost to hire these people and should they be full or part time? How can you get your candidate pool filled?

- How much time and money do you need to set aside for training and education to ensure that you can build a resilient, engaged team?

When you have your overall hiring plan in place, you may find it useful to channel your efforts even more carefully. We all know that you get out as much as you put in. Startups often go at 100 miles per hour and yet nobody has any time. But it's important to **make time** for what's important.

Look at your next twelve months. What type of positions need to be filled within the next six months? Will this be a salesperson to continue to build up a sales funnel and close deals? Will it be a software developer because the product you are creating is nowhere near complete? Is there an individual contributor or expert that you need in your pharma company to create a specific product that's not on the market so far?

Drill down further as this will be helpful to anyone involved in the process, and this is something that needs to be revised and communicated over and over again.

1. Think about which jobs cannot stay open for too long because it will damage your reputation with customers or stifle the development of your product. Can any of them be temporarily outsourced? Can you ensure that none of the company IP is in jeopardy by doing so?

2. Can you cover some of these jobs temporarily internally for a while?

3. Which resources can you mobilise to find the best candidates? Can you establish a budget for advertising, for agencies or use your networks to generate referrals?

4. Identify the most critical roles, that you need to fill regularly, such as your top ten key roles.

The team can now focus their efforts on recruiting for these critical roles quickly, rather than working on forty different roles that need to be filled and spend time in interviews extensively.

The Cost of Recruitment

Arnnon Geshuri (Teladoc Health/Tesla/Google) shared with us different reasons why he believes so many startups fail.

'Pay attention to who you hire, and how that person fits into the team, and aligns with the goals and targets of the company. Is there a match between the company's values and goals and the individual's? The more closely aligned they are, the more a founder can get out of their team and the more the individuals will go above and beyond to fix problems and make sure the company wins and is ultimately successful.

Finding the right person and good hiring starts with finding the right founding team who are aligned to driving the company to success.'

Here are the things people don't tell you when you start a business about hiring, onboarding and working with your teams.

To put things into perspective, a bad hire can cost up to 30% of the team member's potential first-year earnings. Nearly 33% of new hires look for a new job within their first six months on the job. This means that if you need to replace them, it can take you between three and six months to do so, depending on the role, the country you are recruiting in and people's notice periods in accordance with the country law. Some more senior roles can take you up to a year to find a suitable candidate.

The cost is often hidden, not considered and it's stacking up in the end.

- It typically takes six to eight months for a newly hired employee to reach full productivity. Your employee for the first few months spends time learning about the company, products, its people, customers and how the company works internally. They cannot be 100% productive from day one.

- When you hire people, you are also taking time away from the employees who are involved with the actual hiring process, the training and the on-boarding which means they are also not 100% productive. Think about these peoples' salaries on an hourly basis to see the cost. It can be scary but when your processes are efficient it will increase the productivity in the long-term.

- Hires through recruitment agencies can cost you 15-20% of the candidate's annual base salary. Those costs add up if they are with you for less than a year. Agencies are not your enemy, they can, and should be, very helpful. Build solid relationships with them as they can often supply candidates quickly as they understand the market often better than you do, plus they have a database of people who are looking for work.

Leading Interviews

──────────────── Meggy's story ────────────────

Meggy remembers a particular time during the early days of her agency recruitment career.

'I worked on a Marketing Manager role for a large Pharma organisation. There are lots of marketing people in the market, but the company had very specific ideas on the new hire having a specific background, career history and experience.

There was no room for flexibility and this search was made during the pre-LinkedIn era. So, I set out to make my list of target companies. I spent hours and days looking at the candidates registered with the recruitment company to speak to them or to ask for referrals.

I can't count the times where I had made another phone call to a company switchboard just to get shouted at, and have the phone slammed down on me.

It was as if I was going around in circles, my heart pounding every time I picked up the phone, as I was a recruiting youngster back in the day. I remember the type of call centre flair our office had, with recruiters just like me who went in for the chase to find the right candidate, for the right company. I finally had a shortlist of candidates whom I presented to them and they were interviewed by a panel of six over a period of three months, in different stages.

I will never forget the day when I had the feedback call from the HR department of the Pharma company. I was told that none of the four final candidates were any good. I sat at my desk, in the middle of the afternoon with the sun shining on my face, and all was good in the world, until that call came in. I felt sick to my stomach. I had invested so much work, as had the team at the pharma company. It felt like it had all been for nothing.

Putting the phone down, I sat back, put my feelings aside and started thinking. I didn't want to call these candidates and reject them as the feedback wasn't tangible enough. As it was early in my career, it took all my nerve and willpower to go back to the HR person and ask if I could speak with the interview team. After some convincing, the HR person on the other side agreed we could have a conference call.

Of course, it turned out that the people on the interview panel each had different opinions about what this job entailed and what type of person they needed. The questions which were presented to the candidates were all very different, so there was no reference point to rank them.

I decided that now was the time to be cheeky, though this could have gone very wrong. My heart pounding and palms sweating I suggested, 'Why don't you all get together, agree on the role itself and what the person needs to bring to the table immediately and in three to five years time, to be successful. Once we know that we can re-assess *the candidates and potentially ask them back for a final interview with questions which are agreed up front and are the leading questions for every interview.'*

One month later we did exactly that, and one of the candidates was hired and had many successful years in that business.

Help yourself and spare yourself lots of nerves and the time and effort and do it differently, from day one. You don't need to struggle like we did.

─────────────── **Get it right** ───────────────

Standardising your core interview questions for each specific role will allow for a fair recruitment and assessment process for each candidate. And it will help you to fully focus on the person. Engage, listen and be in the moment.

Standardising your core interview questions will help you to create clarity amongst your interview panel, it will avoid repetitive duplicate questions, and allows everyone to have a clear role and part in the interview process.

It is advisable to develop interview questions for each role, though you will be able to use the questions that are related to the company's values for all interviews so you can reflect what's important to the company.

For example:

- Leadership ability

- Strategic foresight

- Communication skills

- The ability to solve problems, work in teams, be resourceful, be calm under pressure, be focussed, be creative – you name it!

You will get the best out of your candidate if you **ask open ended questions**, such as:

Please tell me about your role and responsibilities that you have in your current job, tell me about a time when you had to work in a team, solve a problem with technology, come up with a creative idea, influence your colleague to get a job done.

Or what do you do if you are faced with a task that you have never done before? Have you ever had to do something that you found really challenging, what was it? Why was it challenging and what did you learn?

Have you ever done anything out of the ordinary?

If they struggle to come up with examples in their work environment, ask them about something they solved or created in their private life.

People are multifaceted and some are real doers. Those people who never rest and are always learning are invaluable. Finding them is like finding the needle in the haystack. These people have a growth mindset – and you want them!

You always want to hear about real life examples and how people learn from them. It will also show you if they are capable of reflection.

Sometimes, asking **closed questions** can also be useful, but make sure you know what you are trying to do here. Typically, the answers are short and the candidate may not elaborate unless you prompt them to because closed questions don't lend themselves to expansion. In order to find out more about the person, ask them to elaborate.

Here are some examples:
- Have you ever worked in a different industry?
- Are you comfortable working remotely?
- Do you have much experience with social media?
- Do you give presentations often?

Questions you should *not* ask:
- Age
- Race
- Ethnicity
- Colour
- Gender
- Sex
- Family status/family planning
- Sexual orientation or gender identity
- Country of origin

If you are ever tempted to ask any of these questions, ask yourself how this is relevant to the job.

You may not be thinking about anything when you ask, which year were you born, when did you graduate, how old are you, where were you born, what's your native language, do you have, or plan to have children, how many children do you have, are you sick a lot or do you take a lot of holiday?

However, asking such questions may put the company in a difficult legal position as you could leave yourself open to accusations of discrimination which can have serious consequences. These will damage your employer's brand.

Some candidates may volunteer some of this information and if they do, do not comment on it. Please see example on page 258.

Leadership Team

’ *It's better to have a great team, than a team of greats* ’
Simon Sinek (author, inspirational speaker and corporate leadership consultant and adjunct staff member of the RAND Corporation)

There will come a time when you have hired your co-founder(s) and your first team members and eventually you are starting to look to add more leadership roles to your company to allow your teams to grow and scale.

We get these questions regularly from founders. Once you have managed to attract A-list players, especially within Leadership positions that are a vital to the company, how do you then build a suitable interview process and how does one assess them during interview?

Don't rush this process.

The leadership team that you will hire during your early startup days should be able to move your company forward successfully for at least 3-5 years. Focus on what the company needs not just now, but also in the near and more distant future.

Make sure that you, as the CEO and the Founding team spend time with your Directors, VP or C-level hires over video chats initially to explain more about the role, the company and opportunity you offer. You also want to find out more about the candidate's background and what they are like as a person. Get a shortlist of at least 2-4 candidates that you can meet.

Let them come and see you and the team in your offices. At this stage, every interviewer should be able to assess a different suitability of the candidate and should spend time to explain their role within the company and how they would expect this new role to interact and help them.

And importantly set time aside with your finalist candidate(s) to have some social interaction over lunch or dinner. It's good to see people in a more relaxed setting, rather than a formal interview.

The relationship you develop through the process and the time you spend with them will help you understand the type of person and leader you are about to hire. You need to understand what it is they are good at and where they need to continue to improve, as it will help you to work with your potential management/leadership team in a specific way from the outset.

Do take your time here. It is a two way process after all. The candidate needs to be able to wrap their head around your company needs and its culture. And it will show you if you can work with these people. You want to be able to count on them and call upon them whenever you need to.

Finding suitable people at this level can take a good 6-12 months from the beginning of the search, to when they actually start. That is quite common and often these types of role are open for up to eighteen months.

When you have raised your first seed round, or series A it is good to set some finance aside to get help from an Executive Search company to help you with your senior hire. It sends a couple of signals. It says that obviously you have money, and, most importantly that you are serious and committed to finding an exceptional person for your team.

When you hire for your senior leadership team, if you do not have a fully staffed in-house team, or an experienced recruitment member, use an executive head-hunter. They will help you to understand the candidate landscape and will help you to set up a suitable process.

When you work with an Exec search company, depending on the level of the role, you could end up with an overall hiring fee which is normally paid in three tranches. At the beginning of the search, in the middle and at the placement stage. Investing here, will pay off in the long run.

Assemble an interview team who understand how to handle this process with the highest level of confidentiality. Include some of your board and/or investors at the beginning. Involve key people within your company that this person will work with closely. Take time and care as you do with all your candidates but go the extra mile here and build that personal connection.

Always look for people who are:
- Strategic and forward thinking but still hands on
- Influencers and team players
- Have a good level of humility
- Leadership role models
- Problem solvers

When you interview these people ask them to share their experience, but also their vision for the company and department they will be building with you.

Ask about their biggest successes.
Ask about their biggest failures and learnings.
Ask them about how they motivate and lead teams.
Ask them how they work strategically with other departments.
How do they resolve conflict?
Let them tell you about their team structures.
Let them tell you about their success stories with their direct reports.
Ask them to tell you their failures in managing their team.

Allow them to ask questions to understand your business model and ensure they can show you how they would contribute to the future growth and changes.

Set up a structure and get the most out of every minute of your interviews. Reading this, it might seem like that you have a lot of work to do to prepare for the recruitment process which is probably why so many people don't do it.

Making a bad hiring decision at this level can cost you in so many ways ranging from business productivity to existing relationships with your investors, to low moral within your existing teams ending up with people leaving under the new management.

Top Tips:

- When you offer the job to a person, ensure you get to speak to most of their references.

- When hiring, don't rely on degrees or certificates, what actually matters is the candidate's mindset, drive, collaboration skills and passion for learning, so rather look for 'evidence of exceptional ability'. Because 'if there's a track record of exceptional achievement, then it's likely that that will continue into the future, according to Elon Musk.

- And if you want to know if the candidate is telling the truth, ask them to tell you about the most difficult problems they encountered and how they solved them. The reason for that is – in Elon's words: 'The people who really solved the problem know exactly how they solved it. They know and can describe the little details.'

2.4 – When Things Go Wrong

Consequences

The consequences of a bad hire can be devastating.

Have you ever been in school, at university or work and noticed that one person coming into a group can split the group in half, create a bad vibe within the team, or simply play people against each other?

We've seen it happen when the wrong hiring decision was made.

We all make a hiring mistake from time to time. You will get it wrong at some point. We all have. You have the best intentions during the interview, the candidate does really well, but within weeks or months of them starting, you can see the writing on the wall. It can start with a nagging feeling, and then you see things come to light which you may have feared would happen.

The real impact on the company from a bad hire is that your team's morale will suffer; they may end up working less with each other or spend time on things that keep them from focussing on important goals. Some of your team may need to work more to make up for the person who can't carry the expected workload. As for managers, this could mean more time spent with that one high maintenance person instead of focussing on their overall team and the future vision of the department.

You will lose productivity and, on top of that, you will have the time and cost of having to recruit again.

Action to Take

First, give the new employee a chance. Do you need to spend more time on their onboarding or training? Spend some time listening to them and start having conversations around what it is that isn't working and try to see how it can be resolved together. Give people the benefit of the doubt and see if they can turn things around.

Unless of course your employee has done something that is deemed as illegal, or immoral and not in line with your company's culture. If that is the case, work with a lawyer to remove this person as quickly as possible.

The company's overall goal has priority and if that means removing a member of staff to ensure that the team can continue to press ahead, then so be it.

Once you can really see that this is what needs to happen, don't wait too long. There is never an ideal moment to say good-bye to somebody. Ensure that you go through the legal processes, consulting a lawyer if necessary. You want this process to be handled properly with all necessary steps and paperwork involved so that there is no come back on you or the company in the end.

Have a communication strategy in place for your team and potentially any other parties that need to be informed in a professional, timely manner. Don't take people out and then try and brush it under the carpet. Although this may seem like the easiest route at the time, it will certainly make your team question and wonder what has happened. It may make some people fearful and rumours will start. Worst case they will quietly start to question your leadership capability and then they will start looking for a new job.

Try your best to part company with people in a civil and professional manner from your end, have your company values as well as your employee brand and experience always in mind when you go through this type of process.

Be prepared, however, that this may not be replicated by the person leaving. After all, you need to remain professional, representing your company and the person leaving may be frustrated or disappointed. Don't let that throw you off course, you have a wider team and mission to lead and need to think about what is best for them.

Always remember you will learn from these instances, they will make you sharper and give you a better understanding of what works and what doesn't work for your company, culture and team.

2.5 – Scaling – As You Grow

Team Involvement

Have you heard the phrase 'surround yourself with people who will lift you higher'?

When you build a company that's exactly what you need to do, and you can do this by getting your existing team involved. Great talent knows, and attracts, other great talent.

Remember that a great company isn't just a collection of great people. It's a **team** of great people, working together and pulling in the same direction. That's what culture is all about. It's turning a group of high performing individuals into a team of great people who all agree with the basic principles of *How We Do Things Around Here*. In the end it comes down to trust. If your team and yourself trust each other, it is a great team.

─────────────── Meggy's story ───────────────

Meggy wanted to share a story from her early days in her recruitment career when she worked as a recruiter. She vividly remembers a story of one of her clients, Simone who had worked in Sales for most of her career. She was ace, she smashed her targets and was a natural born leader. Over time she was promoted to Manager and then Director and she ended her career as VP of Sales at a rapidly scaling US Software company, where she worked successfully for several years.

I remember my conversations with her on recruitment. We both knew that average performing sales staff are everywhere, but the rare diamonds, the high performers, are hard to find. High performers are those who go the extra mile, are hands on from the beginning to the end of the sales cycle and are those who speak with the customer and pull the teams together to get the best deal for the company and client. We spent months and months looking at internal applications and reviewing direct applications to the company, in combination with sourcing over social media like LinkedIn, ourselves.

Now don't get me wrong, we found some good people, but we just couldn't seem to uncover the diamond we needed who would be Simone's successor. Four months in, I was speaking with the Purchasing Manager over lunch and mentioned our issue with finding Simone's successor. Within two days, the Purchasing Manager had leveraged his own network from previous companies. We managed to identify two key candidates, one of whom Simone ended up hiring.

When you think about the power of your team's network(s), you need to encourage your people to think about their own network. This is where an **Employee Referral Program(ERP)** comes in.

You can set it up as a basic structure and then scale it. Often in startups, your teams are already naturally referring other great people, but you may not have considered it as a long-term resource.

When your company starts to scale at speed, you should consider all possible avenues to hire great talent, and one of them is to leverage your in-house talent by creating and promoting an official ERP.

Creating incentives for your staff, to introduce people from their network who could fit and add to your culture and company is useful as it will help you to:

- Leverage a network that understands your product & culture
- Reduce your time spent on hiring
- Create a cost effective source of hiring
- Increase retention through better onboarding and training

- Leverage higher offer acceptance rates due to the personal connection
- Most of the time it comes with an inherent cultural match as well as personal bonding due to the existing connection

There are many different ways to create a fair and equal Employee Referral Program. The main tip is to make it as simple as possible for your employees and their referrals to apply.

Establish a structure, communicate it and use an ATS (Applicant tracking system) that allows you to be in line with GDPR and data privacy rules and regulations as you are dealing with confidential information.

Help your teams to focus on the roles which are core to your company, communicate regularly with them and ask for referrals in various ways. Make it fun for them, incentivise them for referring candidates with cash or prizes, be creative but understand what you can do from a financial perspective.

Take matters into your own hands and get your teams involved in hiring. Use your Employee Referral Program (ERP) to shout out where you need help to fill roles. Leverage your team and their powerful network.

Assembling your People Team

You may be wondering when it would make sense to invest in building a dedicated people team. You may still be going through your seed funding, or you may have received your first big series A ticket.

How and when you build your team really depends on your ambition to grow. When you have around 10-20 people, quite often a founding member looks after all people related matters, next to other functions. Typically, that works well. When you start expanding to a team of thirty people, it is time to start looking for a dedicated HR Manager, especially if your plan is to double or triple in size within the year.

If that is indeed the case, you also want to invest in a dedicated Recruiter or Recruitment Manager, especially if your growing ambitions are particularly steep. Both the People and Recruitment Manager will be able to work with you on the long-term strategy which you need to be able to scale, as much as the hands-on requirements to build structures, choose the necessary tools and build their own teams over time.

As with anything, people related matters require focus, just as much as building a product or delivering great customer service. After all your employees are indirectly or directly (depending on how you choose to look at them) your customers. They work for you, with you, on your product and they also have needs and requirements just as your customers would have.

Your Recruitment team will be there to work on anything related from engaging candidates, drawing them into your culture, guiding them through the recruitment process and working strategically on employer branding external, as much as internal.

Your People team looks after your employees from the minute a contract is sent to a candidate, to the time when they convert into an actual employee, then they ensure they get paid on time, and are there to create incentives to support the teams through their whole employee lifecycle.

If you understand how to look at your People function as the function which enables your teams to be at their best, you have just stepped up your game.

Building an outstanding people team, requires the same focus as any other position. When you start to think about hiring a new person into these roles think about the next 18-24 months.

What type of person can bring your startup to a level that can serve your company, depending on the growth rate.

Should they be coming from a specific industry, that is either the same as yours, or a related industry?

Are there companies/brands out there that you admire for their excellent reputation on company culture, if so, is it worth trying to pinch people from these companies?

Does the person have the ability to be hands on, as well as look forward to the next 18-24 months to create programmes, implement systems and processes around the other departments?

You also need to think about how you, as a founder / CEO can keep parts of the people function. For example, you could hire an HR Business Partner and Recruiter who is starting out in their career. You could just add an external, strategic People advisor that will guide you towards achieving your goals and then the team executes them. Delegate as much as you need and want to, as long as you remain involved in the hiring process and informed about what is going on in your people department, which can be seen as the driving force for your culture.

Once you have answered some of these questions, you will have created a baseline for you that will help you to build your desired people team faster.

Your Recruiting Wrap Up

- **Have a plan.** Get your business and hiring strategy in place and aligned.

- **Your people team** is a strategic part of the business: recruiting, onboarding, training, communication.

- **Be laser focussed** on key roles for the company and recruit hard.

- **Always have employer branding in mind,** with everything you do.

- **Act quickly** on any bad hiring decisions.

- **Be flexible,** evolve your plans and scale your processes.

PEOPLE

People are your most valuable
asset. Your employer brand and your
employee's experience make all
the difference.

3.1 What and Why

You as a Leader

Let us start by acknowledging that not every founder considers themselves a leader. Some founders start as programmers, engineers, service providers, experts in their field, entrepreneurs while some are 'ideas' people. Yet, as soon as there are other people involved, they become a leader by default.

Some people struggle with leadership. They struggle to define exactly what it is, what their leadership style is or should be and how they can step up to it. It can be hard for many to navigate the pressures and responsibilities that come with it.

When you are starting a company, dealing with all the associated challenges of finance, bringing your idea to market, sales, operations and all the thousand other things you need to do, your own skills as a leader aren't something you are necessarily always going to think about. But it's an essential element to the success of your company and the culture within it. At the very heart of the culture will be the leader who steers their company with conviction.

Your teams are going to look to you for direction, for vision and a purpose. They will get a sense of achievement simply by you acknowledging their contribution.

Create an environment that fosters equality and opportunities for growth as well as a sense of acceptance and a certain type of security; that's what people are looking for in startups and in their leadership. Being clear on the direction you want to take your company is important as a leader as it sets the tone for everyone involved.

That's why is Leadership is so important. It's not something you can abdicate, even though there are times in every leader's life when they wish they could.

Leaders attract and inspire people to achieve their very best. For all these reasons, you need to actively establish a solid and coherent-public leadership in your company, challenge your own private leadership methods and develop your own personal leadership style right from the beginning.

Purposeful leadership creates meaning, guides decisions, influences behaviour, shapes goals. Direction allows you as an individual and group to remain focussed.

Having a sense of direction promotes better mental health. A clear direction, coupled with purpose and vision is helpful for mental resilience and helps you to achieve your goals, even in the most difficult times.

──────── **There is no culture without leadership!** ────────

A good place to start thinking about your leadership, is by understanding what it is that people are going to need from you and what you need from yourself.

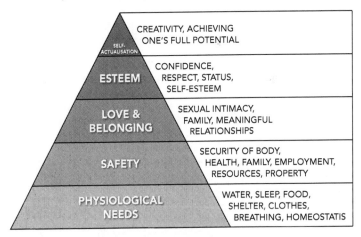

MASLOW'S HIERARCHY OF NEEDS

A useful model is Abraham Maslow's hierarchy of needs. It sheds light on what motivates people and, as a leader, understanding what drives people is essential. Without an understanding, you are just guessing what drives people; with it, you can make educated evaluations and plan, behave and react accordingly.

This sketch on the previous page showcases the motivational theory that Maslow created. The needs lower down the hierarchy must be satisfied before individuals can move higher up.

Definition of Leadership

Leadership takes on many dimensions and encompasses many definitions. Every action or inaction has consequences when it comes to leadership.

There is a real need for entrepreneurial leadership in this world. We face global issues; there are difficult problems to solve that need solution-orientated, creative minds that want to lead towards a common goal.

Think about qualities such as **Growth Mindset**. These are the type of people who are always seeking to learn and have an attitude towards failure that allows them to translate it into something positive – a valuable learning experience rather than something to be ashamed of. When we talk about learning, we mean from keeping up with the latest trends within individual jobs such as the latest engineering or recruiting trends, to learning completely new skills which will allow individuals to move across into different areas from coding to maybe design thinking, marketing, business strategy or others. Growth Mindset also manifests in people who seek to always improve themselves and/or their surroundings. Think about those who work with charities in their own time, raise money through activities, or those who like to improve their own home which allows them to learn and practise new skills. There are those who always seek to self-improve through personal coaching and/or reading books, for example. It doesn't stop there; some people like to learn a new instrument or try different types of sports, or even specialise in something challenging.

Have an open mind and look for people who are so inclined. There is an Austrian saying 'Beim Reden kommen die Leut zamm', which means 'when people get together and talk, things happen'. When it comes to having an open mind, it means being curious about your surroundings, understanding others, putting yourself out there and seeking feedback to understand how you could improve a situation, yourself, or your actions.

We, as humans, are multifaceted. Re-inventing and re-building things and/or ourselves is a key strength of ours. Use it every day. We all hold this power within us. **Be flexible; adapt.**

As a founder and a leader, there are a few key leadership tips that we know will help you to stay resilient and cope with the challenges that are sure to come your way.

Accept that you don't know everything. There's value in learning from each interaction you have with another person. You can't know everything, there are people who have been on the planet longer than you, worked in industries longer than you. Listen and learn and see what makes sense for you; find your path but learn from other people's mistakes. You do not have time to repeat them when you build a startup.

Take time for reflection. Reflect often on things that happen in business and private life and allow the same time for reflection for your teams. It's so easy to get lost in the day to day but it's important that you remain efficient and look ahead.

As a leader it is important that you **create a vision for your company and team**. Share that vision regularly, let people know if the company is heading in the right direction, share with them what the competition is up to, but don't let that drive you. Your goal is what drives you.

We know that some of this may sound repetitive, but we are here to help you prevent the most common mistakes startup founders make.

Facilitate conversations across your organisation and bring people together then step slightly aside to let the minds that you have hired do their work. It is your job to stay high level, look to the future and create opportunities for everyone. It's not your job to micromanage. In fact, it is counterproductive, and it will hinder your company as you go through the stages of growth.

Think big
be bold
look ahead
and take action

But how can you ensure that you display these qualities, and do just that?

Types of Leaders

Leadership is hard, it requires vision, commitment, consistency, the ability to break the status quo, to inspire and lead people. And the first person you need to lead is yourself! That's not always as easy as it sounds but without self-leadership, how can you expect others to follow your example.

We interviewed Paula Leach, who brings years of HR, and Executive Leadership experience with her. We asked her what happens to companies if they are led by an exceptional leader and what happens if the leadership has a more negative influence on the workforce. She explained that Leadership is a choice: it can either be exceptional, mediocre or toxic.

Often, we find accidental leaders in business. As a founder you could have a passion for making a difference or bringing a product into the world. In Corporate organisations, experts are often put into leadership positions. However, these accidental leaders often didn't choose leadership when they got up in the morning. It was something that just came with the territory of promotion, but they aren't always prepared for it and don't always adapt to it well.

You have a conscious choice when it comes to leadership, especially as a founder. If you are a true product person and that is your passion, you don't necessarily need to end up as the CEO. This is definitely something to think about, at any stage of your career and the company's growth.

You can choose to be any kind of leader, every day

Be aware that there are significant performance outcomes, depending on the type of leadership style you choose to pursue.

Exceptional leadership allows people to see the same thing

It's your job as an outstanding leader to ensure that everyone understands what needs to be done to achieve certain goals, both long and short term. But equally, it isn't about dictating to the team; you are there to create conditions that enable clarity for everyone. Allow your team to fail, learn, explore and be creative.

You are here to create a sense of belonging, purpose, engagement and wellbeing for your team. Your job is to be a talent coach and a magnet that people want to engage with.

You are there to do the strategic thinking; be self-aware and have a growth mindset. But most of all, be aware of your ego and contain it to be of service to others. Work on yourself and it will pay dividends. No one likes a leader who has a big ego. Remember the old saying that 'People won't remember what you say, but they'll always remember how you make them feel.'

Mediocre leadership has two characteristics

Often leaders say one thing and do something else, in other words their behaviour doesn't match their words. They can speak about diversity or 'servant leadership' but they are not brave enough to act on it. It creates confusion as your teams may not know how they stand with you. If you do not think, listen, reflect, look forward and are not strategic, you are in a cycle of being reactive, which means letting your actions be dictated by others.

Toxic leadership

Toxic, narcissistic leaders make their environment about themselves. Nothing can exist without them, nothing works well without them.

If their performance and ego rule over everything else, there is no true diversity or innovation. It's a recipe for a single point of failure because your team will, or already has, become passive. Creating a culture of uncertainty or fear means that people will think small and fear failing. They will not collaborate and, at worst, will start blaming everyone else around them. Your company will lose time, innovation, fun, energy and productivity. And at its worst, you as a toxic leader can even make people ill because it's a very stressful environment for everyone to work in. To avoid accidentally becoming a toxic leader you just need to remember the culture principle of *This Is How We Do Things Around Here*; if you don't want your team to behave in a certain way, then don't do it yourself!

Establish your Leadership Skills

In our Purpose chapter, we asked you to work on a few questions, including what sort of legacy you wanted to leave in this world.

I'd like to invite you to take time and imagine sitting on a bench in a park on a sunny day – or go to any other mental safe space you may have created that allows you to think clearly.

Get a pen and paper or secure a space on your desktop to write down your thoughts about your own leadership. Do whatever works best for you.

Here's a few ideas to get you started. Take time to reflect:

- Do you have any successful leaders or role models in your private life, professional life, or that you see and hear about on TV? This could be anything from your closest family, to friends, to TV personalities, to sports individuals or politicians, you name it!

- Now pick the leader (or leaders) you have in mind, or if you have more than one, repeat the next question, over and over again, until you have captured all the information you need.

- What makes the person successful in your eyes, what type of leadership quality do you admire in this person or these people? Do you like their consistency, the way they interact with others, are they always professional or is it their infectious energy and when they speak, is it with purpose, passion and conviction?

Now that you have this information noted down, be brutally honest with yourself. Ask yourself:

- Do you already display some of these leadership qualities and traits?

- If you do, do you really know if the outside world sees you, as you do?

- Have you ever considered asking somebody who is close to you, friend or family, or long-term co-worker or co-founder whom you trust who will be able to give you honest feedback?

- Ask them if they would be willing to help you a little on your leadership journey. Could they tell you honestly what they feel are your key strengths as a person? Be brave, ask them to also tell you what they think you could improve on.

- If you do not feel like you display some of the qualities you value in your role models, what else could you do to learn those? What options/tools do you have available or can make available to learn more? Is it how they speak, their resilience, the ability to keep calm under pressure, the body language they use; what else is there?

Now turn this particular exercise on its head. Think about the worst leader(s) that you have worked with. Or those that others told you about, or people that you see on TV who are classified as leaders and whom you think are hideous or atrocious.

Think about everything you consider unprofessional or unpleasant and anything they display as people or seem to pride themselves on doing that doesn't align with your values; write those things down.

This exercise should give you a better insight into the person you want to be as a leader, and what you do not want to be. Know thyself!

This is a good moment to pause and share with you what Paula Leach had to say about how the company's leadership team and their behaviour impacts on the company culture.

'The leadership team is the company culture, there is no other way around it.

Culture is where decisions are made; culture exists where the ability to set the tone exists. The point of leadership is about creating conditions for people to thrive and move from A to B. Leadership is culture.

Employees reflect the behaviours of their leaders. It is everyone's responsibility within the company to live and carry the company culture into the world.'

Essential Leadership Styles

We asked Bettina Andresen Guimarães who has years of experience in Communications and leads her executive leadership and intercultural coaching business Authentic Wow, to share some of her wisdom with us. Here's what she had to say and it was so powerful she gave us permission to use it in the book.

❝*Leadership is not a personality trait; it is a skill.* ❞ [2]

And yes, it might be one of the tougher-to-learn-ones.

Leadership is a skill that requires a broad spectrum of awareness, openness and willingness to change.

Someone wanting to develop their leadership skills cannot stop at the behavioural level. They need to start by looking at values and beliefs, both their own and those of the people around them. Emotional intelligence, empathy and compassion are strongly associated with the ability to lead – communication does not solely work on an intellectual basis.

One of my favourite quotes in this context is: 'You can become soft in the heart without becoming soft in the head' by Elizabeth Lesser, co-founder of Omega Institute. I am convinced that recognised leaders, consciously or unconsciously, act according to this principle. And while you can, of course, have role models for your own leadership style, ultimately, you must discover and develop your own individual style if you want to lead with personality and authenticity.

Bettina shared with us the three basic essentials of leadership

Leading yourself

If you want to be an effective leader, you have to start with yourself.

How well do you manage your emotions? Do you let them dictate your actions, or do you have the flexibility to choose the state you're in for any given situation? Are you able to focus your energy for the benefit of your mission? Do you have the right mindset to achieve what you set off to do? And do you manage your time effectively, not only for your own sake but also for that of your organisation?

Leading others

There is no ultimate recipe book with the must-haves to lead others.

However, there are some important skills and competencies to have when it comes to motivating others to follow; being capable of building and keeping trust, having and showing honest interest in people, establishing and following clear rules, walking the talk – to name just a few.

Real leadership cannot be decreed. It is granted by those following you.

Allowing others to lead you is an integral part of being a true leader. Having the ability to let others guide you, when necessary, to listen actively and value their expertise, letting them 'brief you on the matter' and make perfect use of the space that you as a leader give them in order to enable them to grow is essential.

Can one lead 'from below'? Of course, you can! Ideally, boss/es will be grateful dealing with someone who is acting responsibly, actively – and smart. Do get me right: leading from below does not mean to 'overrule' someone who is in a senior or higher position. It means taking initiative, exposing others to your information instead of keeping it to yourself. Companies that see this as a resource, an opportunity rather than a threat, will generate new generations of leaders without constantly having to hire them from outside.

'No matter if you had a leadership role before or not, you will have to rethink what kind of leader you want to be in your own company. It is a totally different thing to lead 'a' team in 'a' company than to lead a whole organisation in 'your' company. The latter comes with allowing your team of leaders to lead their teams again. The good thing is that 'leadership is not a personality trait; it is a skill which can be learned, although it might be one of the tougher-to-learn-ones. It is a skill that requires a broad spectrum of awareness, openness and willingness to change.'

Your Leadership Never Ends

Executive Coach and MD of Authentic Wow, Bettina Andresen Guimaraes told us that 'Leadership – as well as good communication – can be learned. I am inclined to say that leadership is the highest form of communication.'

Over your time as a leader, it's good to continue to check in with yourself.

We've already talked about developing your vision of what type of leader you aspire to be, but your leadership journey never stops. It's a good idea to revisit the leadership questions we covered earlier on a regular basis. That's because you will be a very different person in six months' time from the person you are now.

When you undertake your leadership reviews (and even if you are busy, find the time because your leadership skills have more impact on your success than just about anything else in your company), add a couple of extra questions. These simple questions could turbo charge things for you.

Ask yourself:
- What has worked well for you over the year?
- What hasn't worked?
- Have you displayed the leadership style you admire?
- Have you displayed any of the behaviours of the leaders you **didn't** want to emulate?
- When did you display these behaviours? What could you have done differently?
- Is there a need to adapt your leadership style, based on your experience? And if so, what needs to change?
- Are you living your company culture yourself, or just talking about it?

If you don't want to do this by yourself, do it with your Coach, or closest friend or partner. Make sure you choose someone whom you trust completely.

Just a word about bias. Sometimes, people closest to you may have a hard time being impartial, as they subconsciously mean well and don't want to upset you.

Having a third party, who doesn't know you either in private or in work, may be the better option.

There are so many amazing coaches and mentors out there, it never hurts to surround yourself with a variety of good people you can call on.

Try your best to develop a self-awareness of your leadership style and the impact it has on your direct teams, your company and customers. It will make you a better leader.

When we arrive in this world, our actions affect others. We can easily think that our lives belong to us only and that we can do what we want. But that's not the case, as you will have surely seen throughout your own life.

Every interaction you have, changes somebody's life for the worse, or for the better.

In the end, you choose how you want to walk through this life. Just remember, that each step takes you into somebody else's world.

As a leader, you will have to make decisions that are unpopular with some, because it is your job to look after a variety of people within your company. But how you do it will make a difference.

How you think and behave will either help you gain in confidence, or turn people against you. As a leader, be sure to walk with purpose, on a clear path and take people with you.

As part of your role as a leader, it is important to understand from day one how to develop leadership in others. It's important for many different reasons.

You want to ensure longevity, create more leaders who may be able to move into other roles or companies in the future and affect more lives positively thanks to your leadership and guidance.

Ensure that your company can be run in your absence. You are the type of leader who looks ahead, creates vision, sets directions but leaves their team the room to create, develop themselves and feel fulfilled in their work and contribute to the mission and vision of the company. If you can't do that, you aren't being a leader, you have just created a high-pressure job for yourself!

We, as humans, are never a finished article. If you stop innovating yourself, you will stifle your own growth, and everyone else's.

Through the Coronavirus pandemic we have seen that change is possible, at a fast and vast scale. It's fundamental to human survival. We have a responsibility to change our consciousness to see the world, our planet and each other differently and allow us to inhabit the earth as one.

Ask yourself how you want to come across, and what feels authentic to you.

There is something very powerful you need to know and realise; only you, yourself can lead with integrity and conviction. You are, or can be, the one to show people the way to go, but also where to draw the line.

Paula Leach shared with us what advice she would give to any leader:

 Find space to think. Really reflect, create space for learning and reflection.

--------------- **Mareike's story** ---------------

Mareike wants to share a story about reflection.

In a previous company I had a colleague who had an awesome habit. Every day, he would first eat a prepared lunch with his colleagues, to spare the time queuing up at the local canteen, and then he would excuse himself to go outside into the little court and meditate for 10 minutes. When it rained, he would find a free meeting room. I can tell you, he managed to always remain calm, reflective and decisive in any given situation, which made him a respected, admired and very much liked leader. He was one of those people everyone seemed to like working with and projects went smoothly when he was involved. People looked up to him. Of course, you could argue, that it could have simply been his talent or personality trait, but what if it wasn't? What if his talent was forged by this habit? What is the worst that could happen if you tried it out yourself? You might lose some time you could have spent on what? Eating? But the best case would be, that you gain an inner strength, a resilience and train your self-refection muscle. I think, it's a no-brainer.

Ask questions and listen hard. It's a privilege to be a leader and have people join you and your eco system. Out of respect for yourself and others, allow yourself time to understand your actions, behaviours and how you come across in this world.

Most importantly, have fun.

When it's not fun for you, it's also not fun for anyone around you.

A word of advice from Boryana Straubel (Generation Collection & Straubel Foundation):

'Always focus on your overall goal, and work towards it step by step, every day without fail. Show up every day for everyone as the professional that you are. Think about what legacy you want to leave in this world.'

Action and Commitment

'Make a contract with yourself! Write down, what you value, what you stand for as a leader, what you will fight for, and what you are willing to sacrifice.' – Ralph Suda (multiple founder, business angel and advisor)

There is power in any leadership role, so use it wisely. Your actions can let a product, people and ideas flourish, or you can dominate and suffocate it and them, to suit your own ego.

Walk the talk, don't think that 'window dressing' on certain matters, such as diversity or sustainability for example, will wash for very long. People see through such things. Limited action will not give you any long-term following, either external or internal. In a startup, and arguably in any size of company, you want a team that is focussed on outcomes and accountability.

Arnnon Geshuri, (ex E-Trade, Google, Tesla and current CPO of Teladoc Health) had a conversation with us around the topic of what essential skills founders need to succeed.

You need to be persistent. There will be stumbling blocks, heart aches and failures but you need to stay strong. Show resilience, give reassurance, show calmness even in the most difficult of circumstances. Stay laser focussed on the business, the model, and how you want to go to market. Know your strengths and weaknesses, it will help you to fill in the blind spots. Learn how to hire, lead, develop and train effective people. Make people want to stay. Be a good people manager, listen to your staff and don't micromanage. Build connections with employees on vision, connect your employees to each other, to their job and to the overall mission.

Create a culture of learning. Are they learning skill sets that will help them in their professional career for vertical learning? Lateral learning is equally important. Encourage learning for self-improvement and personal growth. What makes you a better person? Is it yoga classes, self-improvement or what?

Don't just focus on results, focus on the actions that produces results.

Always remember that your focus determines reality.
Without commitment, nothing happens.
Commitment is an act, not a word.

Arnnon and Ralph have really valuable insights and points.

So, knowing how to engage, motivate and leading your team's is a real gift. It's no secret that people who are passionate about what they do, and that work under favourable conditions will be more productive and successful. Even if you and your teams' day to day work gets hard – and it will – they still have the motivation, drive and tools to overcome adversity if you set them up in a good way. All it takes is commitment, focus and leadership.

Top Tips:

- Get yourself a mentor(s) to develop your professional journey

- Find a coach who works with you on your leadership & personal development

- Create a set of behaviours for your leadership team that you deem as acceptable and unacceptable in relation to your company culture, train them and hold them accountable

On a final note on leadership, we love the creativity of Bumble (the dating app where women are in charge of making the first move) when it comes to employee satisfaction and retention.

In June 2021 the company temporarily closed all its offices for a week to combat workplace stress. 700 staff worldwide were told to switch off and focus on themselves for one week with a paid vacation in June.

Whitney Wolfe Herd, the founder of Bumble, told media that the reason for this drastic measure was that the company had

had a busier year than most firms, with a stock market debut, and rapid growth in user numbers.

This is very modern leadership; focussed on the goals, but knowing what people needed. This is what Whitney was willing to do, and what most business leaders would not have done. After such a busy and successful year, with people under a great deal of stress, can you imagine just how powerful it was to do something like that. It was a great way to show people that they are appreciated. It's a demonstration of human centric leadership.

The lesson? Treat people like you would like to be treated, be focused and set new standards. Don't be a follower when you can be a leader.

3.2 – How to Set It up

Prepping for Success

When startups begin to scale up, they can quickly descend into panic and chaos, especially when it comes down to hitting targets.

Leadership and good foundational structures that make your company effective are of the essence.

As a founder and leader, and as a company, it is vital to ensure you get the legal and mandatory obligations right. If you get this right from the beginning, it will help you with your due diligence when you fundraise.

Trust us, this will come up and it is a really important point.

Many founders don't think of this. They hustle hard, sweat and even cry when they have to pull everything together quickly for things like annual audits, tax returns and investor due diligence. It sounds dry, we know. It's not the glamourous part of founding a company, but it is a part of a founder's life. There's no way of getting around it.

It's critical that you make time for these, often boring, activities on a regular basis, so you don't fall behind on something important or get caught out when you are asked for the details by a regulatory body, tax authority, or potential investor.

Has it happened to you, or have you heard about it from founder friends where the whole team has had to pull 'all-nighters', and work for days and even weeks to pull certain information together for a due-diligence process, or an audit? With anxiety rising in your team, and with tired faces, exhausted from little sleep these experiences are stressful for everyone involved, but you can make it a lot easier for everyone.

We have got you covered so you can help yourself and your teams.

Here are a few things we think you should consider to make sure you are not caught out.

Top Tips:

- Get your important contracts and legal documents in order to ensure that you are operating under the rules and regulations of the country where your offices are based and keep them in a safe place. These should cover supplier & partner contracts, employment contracts, IP documentation, NDA's, payroll, and all insurance documents and so on.

- Make sure your financial paperwork is all in order. Regarding taxes, always be prepared for due diligence and other audits so implement a system online and offline and be sure to keep accurate version control of important documents and ensure only a minority in your company have access to them.

- Bring yourself up to speed and create structures internally for governmental and legal regulations: inclusion and anti-discrimination, GDPR, the new AI act in Europe, Health and safety, Covid 19 measures or the general law.

Set up for Resilience

When you go from a company of five people up to around fifty, guidelines or systems are created or implemented as and when necessary. But when you start scaling quicker than you thought, you need to keep a balance between offering structures to create a fair and equal working environment which needs to be set within certain legal parameters, and over processing and documenting everything just for the sake of it.

Lisa Bodell, Future Think CEO, who ranks amongst the Top fifty speakers worldwide shared tips with us on life hacks for founders.

'You may want to say Yes to everything but as a result, you will lose your focus.

This is where simplicity comes in; define meaningful work, define how it ties into organisational purpose and what you want to say No to. You need speed.

As a founder, give people permission to not do more, but to do less.

Avoid large company syndrome: getting caught up in policies, procedures and unnecessary work and stupid rules.'

Lisa was happy to share with us what she believes makes businesses successful when they shift their culture to focus on innovation and apply simplicity.

'Innovation will focus you not just on who you are today but who you are becoming. Successful people are not just focussed on today but also on tomorrow, it keeps them ahead of the competition.

Applying simplicity is important because it is the front end of innovation. Everyone thinks that the front end of innovation is ideas. It isn't, it is having the time to think.

Most people would love to do it, it's not that they can't do anything, but they are drowning in meaningless work. Often, they are spending all their time in meetings or on email.

Simplicity will help you pivot to meaningful work. It will help you to focus; it will give you speed.'

Top Tips:

- Run short effective meetings with an agenda and follow up plan

- Create the essential structures and guides every company should have

- Revise structures and processes regularly to see what's redundant; keep it simple and slick.

Longevity

If we take you back to your hiring process for a second, to your open roles; you may have already struggled to find the right person who could add to your culture and bring much needed skills to the team.

Let's take building a company that requires software teams as an example. Software people are sought after by the majority of companies.

According to a study by EDC, there will be approximately 27.7 million software developers by 2023 across the world. A Forbes article in 2021 revealed that there are over 920,000 unfilled positions for software engineers in the U.S. alone, with only 165,000 potential applicants. And this isn't the only skills shortage we have in the world.

How can you set up for longevity and sustainability in your workforce which allows you to scale and remain competitive?

Your initial thought may be that you need to scale fast now and that you don't have time to train anyone, right? So why are we talking about long-term then?

Well, that's two-fold.

First – when companies grow fast, they have a tendency to burn their people into the ground quickly. Your team members could become sick or leave you altogether.

Second – you don't get around to planning ahead for certain departments, roles and skillsets anymore, unless you can throw copious amounts of money around for salaries, perks or sign on bonuses for hard to fill roles.

When you think about your company culture, and the future consider:

Are you encouraging lifelong learning and sponsoring your employees' learning?

Should you provide mentors or coaches for your staff for their personal development?

Should you provide specific leadership training to ensure a consistent leadership team?

Would you be able to create rotation opportunities within certain departments for recently appointed graduates or apprentices who just finished their education, so you get them early? They would start in a particular role but are given the opportunity to experience other departments so they understand all aspects of the business. This way you, and they, will discover many hidden strengths and be able to utilise them better.

Should you provide flexible working hours for your staff?

Should you be flexible on their work location?

Should you create job shares for some roles, so that in future you have a possibility to turn them into two full time experienced employees?

Up-skilling your workforce has always been important, but a life-long learning mindset, combined with resilience will be a necessity in the future. The ability to influence people and build relationships with your teams will be essential. By enabling your team members, you provide possibilities for yourself, and them, which you may not have seriously considered previously.

3.3 – Getting Up and Running

Employee Experience

You will have heard us mention the words Employee Experience a few times already and we will look at this more closely now. Getting this part right will elevate your startup, to the next level and ensure that you are creating the right platform for highly effective teams.

You, as much as your team, experience the world of work in certain ways. As a company, you can actively shape the experiences your teams have today as well as in the future.

You may have hired your first 20-40 or more people and think that's it. We did it, they can get to work and will love being here forever.

As you are reading this book you may think, my people won't leave me. Things are great as they are now. But the reality is that you have hired ambitious people, and they have ambitions of their own, such as career progression, a certain financial status or independence, and even learning new skills. It could be any or all of the above. When you realise this fully, simply create a place where your current and future employees can grow and develop their skills, then they will grow with you for quite some time and not be tempted to run off to the first place that offers them what they need.

──────────── **Antonia's story** ────────────

Antonia joined a software startup that was focussed on employee wellbeing. At the time she joined, the company had just raised 15M EUR during its series A round and the team was twenty people strong.

Her interview was super, she got to meet at least eight

key people within the company during the process and had already reached back out to them in her first week of work and re-connected with them. There was a real buzz and positive energy across the company after the funding round.

She was surprised somewhat when she noticed within her first month that the company spent all their efforts solely on the product. They had good parties, Pizza Thursdays and meetings in the park, that was great. But there was no technology whatsoever around employee connection and experience, apart from Slack.

Her role was to build the HR/People function as this had been managed by one of the co-founders so far. She was ecstatic as she was able to come up with various solutions and options together with the founders that would provide a great platform for their employees to be connected, engaged and informed about people related topics as well as company and industry updates.

Antonia ensured that an ATS (Applicant tracking system) was purchased that allowed candidates to get more insight into the company and enable them to interact with the teams more seamlessly. The team internally welcomed this change as all CV's and relevant data was in one system, easy to review and collect interview feedback from everyone. And they were finally able to get data to see what was happening with each role. Recruitment hadn't been easy for a while and it helped them understand where they received hardly any applications, or where the interview process was too slow.

She also asked for budget to implement a suitable HRIS (Human Resources Information System) to hold all private employee data. Both the ATS and HRIS system need to be GDPR compliant, this was already a relevant tick box. The HRIS system finally allowed them to approve and *track holiday taken by the team, to communicate more seamlessly on contracts, to create surveys across the company and gather relevant feedback, all in one place. Antonia chose a system that also allowed for employee interaction like an intranet where they could share the most important documents for the team to review, as well as company updates and social information. As a result, the team felt a lot more connected and felt that there was a lot more transparency and a more up to date information flow.*

And that was just the start, she looked into salary structures for the current and future team to ensure that they can remain competitive now and in the future. She investigated perks and benefits for the teams, on top of all the nice social things the company already did and most importantly she looked for a good learning and development tool and coaches to help existing employees to improve their skills. As this company was focused on employee wellbeing as a product, part of their culture was recognition and celebration.

She found just the right tool which enabled people to give each other feedback, it was just what they needed. It was interactive, quick and simple. The team was able to analyse the data for each employee now and in the future.

She created a great employee experience that could be changed and adapted whenever needed. This team understood that treating your employees as customers, helps you remain innovative and respond to feedback fast and keep your finger on the pulse of what your internal customers' needs are.

All these systems we mentioned above will allow you to work with a company of ten people or more. Choose a system that works for your company for the next 12-24 months and will allow for scalability.

Technology and systems are one part of your employee experience. The other part is how an employee can experience their own personal growth within the company.

Onboarding

Onboarding is part of your employee experience and employer branding. You never get a second chance to make a first impression. During your onboarding phase this impression counts more than ever.

At many companies, people think onboarding is something that happens on the day that a new team member joins the company and the first few days after, maybe a week max. Let's look at this more closely as you are missing out on an opportunity to build your culture and retain your best people otherwise.

At Lilium, we looked at onboarding as an important part of the company culture from day one. The aim was to make new hires feel welcome, connect them to their peers and senior stakeholders within the company and to really ensure they get a feel for the company's vision, mission, tools and processes.

It was all about creating an effective introduction to the company to set up employees for success.

Now, most of the time, a good onboarding process can appear as if it happens all on its own, probably because people tend to only notice when things go wrong. Most things that are well designed to reduce friction have a habit of going unnoticed. However, occasionally people DO notice.

Back to Lilium.

One day the People team received a thank you note from a recently joined team member. It was around the three-month anniversary of them joining and they dropped over an email. In the email they explained to us how much they appreciated all the company's efforts, from the recruiting process to the call from their manager prior to their first day, the well-designed welcome pack they received that included company clothing to the on board-postcard, signed by all respective team members.

This new team member explained to us that they loved how we set up the first few weeks with relevant meetings, lunches and social events as well as the obligatory business meetings to ensure that they were set up for success. For someone to notice is great, but just think how much loyalty they must have felt to the company and to their team members to want to put that into writing.

In larger companies you will often be shown tools, processes, policies. You will be introduced to how the company works, collaborates and communicates. You will often be immersed in the company history and its culture, what's expected of you as an employee and what's expected of you to work towards the overall company's goal. So why would you not, as early as possible, set things up so that you do this from the beginning, and scale it as you grow.

We have spoken to founders and leaders who believe that onboarding only lasts for two weeks. Studies have shown that it takes up to eight months for a new team member to reach full productivity, and it can take up to two years until they are fully productive.

The science behind the power of psychology is out there and readily available for you to investigate online.

- 69% of employees are more likely to stay with a company for at least three years if they experienced great onboarding.

- Organisations with a standard onboarding process experience 50% greater new-hire productivity.

For us, onboarding starts from the day you interview your potential new team member and continues as they go through the whole offer process and then join the team. How the CEO, Leader, or Manager communicates between the offer and their first working day, makes a real difference. It's also about the support you give during their first weeks and months.

And during those first days and months, you can really make a difference by creating a fun and interactive onboarding process. The best way for an adult to learn is if they are surrounded by like-minded people, when they feel that information is relevant to them and they have activities and assignments the same as when learning at school. If you manage to connect them emotionally, and if they understand the benefits of your product and service during the onboarding process, then your employee will be off to a productive start. They will get up to speed quicker than in other companies where new employees need to find out everything for themselves. Have a look at our Onboarding checklist which we created for you in the back of this book on page 259.

Onboarding starts with your first employee and should never end.

Facilitate connections and let them thrive.

Top Tips:

- Use this opportunity and connect your new employees to people they will work with regularly.

- Immerse people in your culture and in *How You Do Things Around Here.*

- Give them time with the Founding team and/or the CEO, in the form of a team presentation or one to one meetings. Especially during your company's early days. Make it scalable.

Guidelines and Policies

Through Mareike's research and our combined work experience, we have noticed that where there is a group of people, it's inevitable that there will be issues amongst the team members, between them and their managers, or vice versa. There could be inequality in how holiday is approved, or how promotions are given to cases of harassment, or even gross misconduct. Sometimes, there may be more than one, and even several, issues going on at once. It happens when founders least expect it, and sometimes from the people they least expect it from.

How you choose to prepare for, behave and respond in these situations is a completely different matter.

You always want to empower your teams, trust them and instil responsibility in everyone. Create a space where people worry less about bureaucracy and focus more on what's important. But equally you want to create a baseline of fairness and protection, in case you need it. Just as you would as a parent, looking after your children.

When you wrap your head around that, whatever you do, you are always acting from a leadership position and as the voice of the company, it is good to embrace your company's values and communicate in accordance with those values.

So, when you think about setting up basic guidelines and policies, it's helpful to know in advance that inevitability is just that; inevitable. This is the way to keep it meaningful, to the point and not overcomplicate things. You can see lots of examples of types of policies on the internet so look at some to give you a starting point and then choose which aspects suit your purpose.

Top Tip:

Start with a well written **Code of conduct**, which is a set of policies outlining the norms, rules, and responsibilities within your company. It goes a long way. It allows your employees to understand how to interact, and how your company expects them to behave – on your behalf. You can expand your code of conduct as you grow, start with the basics such as security, safety, holiday and absence, harassment and complaint procedures, etc.

Your Code of conduct will help you to:

- Set standards and expectations for behaviour that everyone is expected to follow
- Create a level of uniformity in terms of rights and responsibilities of all team members
- Address legality and ethical safety
- Make informed decisions
- Let customers and partners know how you operate, what you value and where you draw the lines they can work out if they

want to work with you – creating a level of transparency for a healthy business relationship

If you don't want to initially create full-blown policies, simple guidelines will do just fine in the beginning. Once they exist, they can easily be transformed into official policies.

The company, CharlieHR, used to have an unlimited paid annual leave policy, but they scrapped it. Not because people were taking advantage, but for the exact opposite reason: people weren't taking enough time off! Team members knew they had as much time as they wanted, they just didn't get round to taking it. They also found that people who could afford to do cool things while they were off took more than those who couldn't afford holidays or lots of days out with the kids – so a gap started to grow between those who took the time they wanted and those who didn't. And the people working more days had to cover for those who took more time off.

What started off as a dreamy view of creating a great place to work, and treating people like adults, became a two-tier system and the 'unlimited' concept caused people anxiety. There was no indication of what was acceptable. No boundaries. That confused people. When they surveyed their team, people said things like:

'I always felt a little nervous asking for time off because I wasn't really sure if I was asking for too much – I didn't know what the norm was.' and *'I remember wondering whether I was taking the mick... and what other people across the company would think of my usage? I felt like I was somehow doing something against the best interest of the company and my team-mates.'*

So, think carefully about setting boundaries. A lack of them, even if backed with good intentions, can backfire. CharlieHR scrapped the 'unlimited holiday' policy and people felt much more comfortable taking the time they needed within a new set allowance.

The policies we recommend having in the early phase of your company are:

- Health and safety policy
- Equality policy/ harassment policy
- Working Times, Absences and Holidays policy
- Data protection policy
- Internet and social media policy

Other areas where it helps to have some guidelines are on how to manage and run effective meetings, how to collaborate such as folder structures and naming conventions and how to give feedback.

Team Structures

As your company keeps growing, more clear positions and departments will form naturally as a result. Sometimes you need to create them deliberately otherwise you take the risk that people will be working on the same, or similar projects, not knowing what each of you is doing.

You will want to ensure that people understand who to speak to about certain areas and projects within the company.

Therefore, creating some sort of internal and external structure is inevitable. You need to make it simple for external people to identify who they need to speak to, and with every hire you make, you are sending a signal to the market.

When you start a company, life is different. It's not just about the chase and thrill of getting going and keeping going. It's often also about surviving from one day to the next.

Every day is spent chasing down the next customer, dealing with relationship management or developing or fixing a problem you encountered. It can be both exhilarating and stressful. How you structure the roles can make all the difference to how stressful it's going to be in the longer term and how much energy you have for the really important stuff.

The common notion is that every startup, maybe with a few exceptions, needs three people to be operational and efficient: a designer, a developer and a marketeer. Or as Rei Inamoto, chief creative officer for AKQA put it:

> *To run an efficient team, you only need three people:*
> *a Hipster, a Hacker and a Hustler*

The designer (or Hipster) is not only the artistic creative mind but also the technical designer, constructor and creator of processes. They are concerned with the human aspect of a problem and most likely the person to take over the culture and communication element in the early stages. They are also the person to challenge the status quo and see the bigger picture. The designer combines the personalities of a dreamer and an innovator.

The developer (or Hacker) sees problems and knows how to develop solutions for them. They have a solution-oriented mindset and the skills to implement the solutions, as well as the technology behind an idea. The developer is a doer and taskmaster at heart.

The marketer (or Hustler) knows how to reach a target group, is communicative and social. They are the sales person who likes to satisfy customers and is the driver of the performance of the whole team. They know how to spark and inspire others. The marketer connects the whole team with the vision.

If the first three people in your startup don't match these three roles, lack some skills, or if your founding team already consists of four, then make sure the skills of those three types are evenly distributed amongst them, or get a fifth person on board, who will cover any missing skills.

In this phase of defining and assigning the roles, everyone needs to cast aside their pride and take the role they are best suited for.

The charismatic, visionary, communicative entrepreneur should be the CEO, even if this is not the founder who had the initial business idea.

When those three (or five) roles reach the limit of their capacity and you need specialisation in another field, you should have a personnel plan ready, laying out which skills you need by when and in which area.

Ralph Suda, Multiple Founder, Investor and RSC Consultant for founders told us about his experience. *'At the beginning it is good to have some generalists with the required core skills rather than all specialists in your small team. Generalists can cover a lot of things outside of their core skill zone with potential for excellence and further growth. Specialists are often too focused on one single field of expertise and, at this point you cannot hire one person per field. You need people who can see beyond their own noses, see the need to do something in another field and put that additional hat on whenever the need arises.'*

Prof. Claas Triebel (Perform Plus &Growth Academy) adds that as soon as an area or task becomes too big and needs in-depth development, you can hire a specialist to take over and move the generalist to a new area. This suits many generalists who even appreciate it, because they simply don't want to specialise and 'get stuck' in one small niche of expertise.

So, how will you know whether someone wants to specialise in a field and grow into the niche of expertise, or switch roles internally regularly, connect departments and fields and remain rather generalist in their role?

Ask them! Get feedback and operate an open door policy.

3.4 – When Things Go Wrong

Difficult Situations and Conflict Management

We want to encourage you to leverage your culture in everything you do. Even when you are finding yourself in unforeseen or difficult circumstances or conflicts. With all things culture ownership is key.

Conflict happens when people feel that they are being treated unfairly, that they are discriminated against or that management is poor. Conflict often starts due to a lack of communication and in some cases it creates confusion. People will work towards their own priorities if there isn't a clear objective set out and this can create distrust amongst staff as many may suspect there are hidden agendas.

When different backgrounds and working styles are brought together misunderstandings can happen and trigger difficult situations.

Paying attention and resolving conflict is the key to reducing the negative impact this can have on individual team members, the team itself or the whole company.

If you don't address it, your employees' productivity will decline, confidence in the team or leadership may disappear, people could lose their self-esteem. The stress and anxiety of a difficult situation will most likely result in more sickness, depression and absences and in some cases even a legal dispute. Depending on how disgruntled the team member is your company's reputation could even suffer.

Conflict often leaves both parties in a position where they feel vulnerable and unprotected. Along with everything else you need to do as a company, you must have consideration for the

167

human element and emotions throughout this process.

In whatever way you want to approach this topic of conflict management, it should be aligned and anchored in your company culture. Make it a management focus to proactively manage any conflicts in the future.

——————————— **Anna's story** ———————————

Anna worked for a company that had scaled up to sixty people. Things had gone well for the first two years for the team. Now they had made profits for the first time and had available cash, they hired more people and so pressure started to increase to deliver a better product and service.

As they added more staff, they eventually encountered a 'near miss' situation where two employees were going through a very difficult time with each other and nearly resigned.

Anna the leader of the team at the time, managed to defuse the situation by having regular conversations with the staff members and creating clearer lines of responsibility areas within the team.

The founders and teams where really shaken up by this, as they had never spent a minute thinking about conflict situations until then. Why would they? The team was harmonious and focussed so far.

They knew that it was time to think about how to deal with difficult situations in a more structured way. The company had a very open, feedback culture so they asked the team to see if there would be a group of volunteers that want to establish 'conflict resolution principles' along with suggestions on how to reinforce them, in accordance with the company's culture. Four of her employees came forward. After some brainstorming and researching, they

*established five principles. It was an important step for the
company and team.*

*They created a guide with a short video for internal use
on how to promote what they called 'the five resolution
principles' frequently during their regular companywide
meetings. They also built this into the onboarding
programme as feedback and communication was at the
heart of their cultural values.*

—————— **Here are their conflict resolution principles:** ——————

1. **Address the problem** and not each other. Be fair and
   investigate what the root causes are and do so together and
   not in public.

2. **Listen actively** to what is said with words as well as by
   observing intonation and body language. Take the other's
   point and weigh up their arguments. Don't take it personally.

3. **Don't blame others.** Accept your share of the responsibility if
   applicable, for a beneficial outcome.

4. **Set clear expectations.** Each party needs to understand what
   is required from them in order to move forward.

5. **Use direct communication.** Say what you mean and mean
   what you say and remove emotions. You are acting on behalf
   of the company and its people. As an employer stay away
   from 'I-messages'. Back things up with logic and fact.

6. **Focus on the outcome.** Be solution-oriented and open minded
   but act on behalf of the company even if that means there are
   no solutions, for example, if an employee assaulted somebody
   or stole from the company.

It's also important to have an external law resource at your disposal too. Ensure that you follow the right steps to do the best for the employee in their circumstances, but also make sure that your company is covered from a legal and compliance perspective.

Working together as closely as you do in a startup inevitably causes friction now and then. And this can be a good thing. If the nature of a conflict is constructive and professional, it means, people care enough to fight for it, they take your company vision seriously and 'own' their tasks. When people dare to challenge the status quo and each other, it can be good because it takes trust and respect to disagree openly. It also means they feel confident and comfortable enough to speak up and stand their ground.

But disputes are only constructive and valuable if all parties intend to reach a beneficial outcome over the issue at hand - and if they get along on a personal level. On the other hand, destructive and personal conflicts are dangerous for your company if they aren't taken seriously and dealt with swiftly and professionally.

So, how can you ensure that potential future disputes are constructive and fruitful?

How can you prevent personal and destructive conflicts, or at least keep them from boiling over?

There are different approaches to managing and solving conflicts. These range from being accommodating, through avoidance, compromising and competing, to collaboration. Every approach is a valid one, depending on your company culture. And one of the most important things we can tell you is that under no circumstances should these types of meeting be played out in public. If meetings turn unprofessional, it will affect the morale of everyone surrounding them.

It depends on the culture and nature of the people who are having the disagreement, the personal management style of the mediator, and the nature of the conflict itself for how it will be resolved.

In the chapter on communication culture, we address different types of communication, which will help you evaluate and decide upon the most appropriate conflict management approach that you can use in order to make your conflict resolution principles known and keep them present in people's minds.

BUT IN GENERAL, HERE ARE MORE TIPS:

Nominate or vote for a conflict manager or trusted person, who will take care of keeping the principles alive, communicating them regularly and coming up with more ways to practise them. This person can also function as a confidant or mediator for team members who want or need external mediation during a dispute.

A mediator or trusted person is also a great solution for occasions when a quarrel is a personal one or has no objective root cause, which can then be resolved professionally still sticking to your principles.

At a later stage, you might want to think about hiring an external professional mediator on demand, who can help in any given situation. Alternatively, you can explore professional training you could offer your employees and make someone from your team an internal mediator, who you will then train professionally just like you need to train fire wardens and first aiders.

Let's take a company in Germany as a living example.

In Germany, any company with more than five employees is obligated to allow their employees to establish a works council. This council would take over any personnel problems and conflicts and could also help with personal quarrels if required since members of the work council:

- **Are bound by confidentiality**
- **Act in the role of work council member and not as colleagues, thus would be acting professionally**
- **Have the best interest of the employees in mind**
- **Have been voted on ensuring they are trusted colleagues.**

But let's be open and honest here: a work council will also have to be trained and must be allowed to consult external consultants, which your company must pay for. Additionally, employees working as council members need to be exempt from their day to day job for a certain number of hours per month, which means a slight reduction in their productivity. As a result, many German founders shy away from working councils. But they cannot prevent their employees from founding one and should start thinking about facilitating one with their employees whilst the team is small because at that point, establishing one is still relatively cheap and you are still on good terms with everyone. So, it's more likely to be a collaborative relationship between management and the work council. Of course, in other countries this would be a matter of choice, but one you might think is worth contemplating.

If you wait and try to avoid this topic for financial or investor attractiveness reasons, your employees might start a working council (or similar process) once they are dissatisfied with your management and the atmosphere has turned hostile.

There are also external Employee Assistance Programmes (EAP) services you can offer to your employees as part of your benefits programme. During the Covid-19 crisis, 78% of all US American companies provided EAP to their employees.

An EAP is an external service providing free professional and confidential assessments, short-term counselling, referrals and follow-up services for employees. Employees can call on them for both personal and work-related problems. Benefits of EAP are that employees can contact a qualified psychologist or consultant directly and get a quick response. Furthermore, the conversations are totally confidential and will have no impact on the employee´s relationship with their manager, colleagues and/or subordinates. There is a twenty-four-hour hotline to offer support at any time. Of course, this is yet another cost you would have to bear and this kind of benefit might only make sense at a later stage. But we want you to know that these things do exist so you know all your options to help prevent or resolve problems, manage conflict and difficult situations which will, in turn, help you to keep your team healthy, happy and productive.

As with anything in life, treat people how you want to be treated – keep it professional and with the utmost confidentiality.

—— Communication is key under these circumstances ——

If you ever find yourself in a position that you have to say goodbye to one of your team, the first thing you must do is consider everybody involved.

This includes the person leaving, the rest of the team, and yourself. You will need to come up with a methodical way of explaining what has happened for your remaining employees. Get together with the team members who worked closely and regularly with the person who is leaving. Inform them of the situation as well as what the next steps are, including re-recruiting, or explaining if you need to split the workload across the team.

You may want to take time for some 1:1 meetings, to approach key employees that this person may have interacted with regularly but who does not sit in that team. Have a conversation with both privacy and professionalism in mind for everyone.

Having guidelines/policies on how to behave during these circumstances will be helpful and transparent for your whole company. Always work with your HR/ People team or an external adviser who understands employment law.

Harassment and Discrimination

Imagine some time from now when you may be in the position to celebrate with your team. This could be a Christmas party – or if you have made a conscious decision to steer away from religious references call it a Winter party – let's say, where you want to review the year, celebrate successes and reflect on what could be done better.

Imagine you walk into the most amazing venue that has been hired especially for you and your team. Everyone is exhausted from the year, but happy and in good spirits having a great party to celebrate with colleagues and friends. You hear the music blasting from the speakers, the sound of glasses raised, the food being eaten, the laughs and the good times. Smell the air that's warm and smell the smells of smoke machines (let's imagine your DJ has them) and see all the people mingling with glasses in their hands, enjoying their drinks.

Thoughts don't turn to harassment in this case, but unfortunately these events all too often lead to such cases in many a company. We have all heard of the terms Harassment and Discrimination and we all know they are bad things which should be avoided at all costs. We strongly assume that we all don't want to harass anyone or discriminate against anyone, especially when you are about to build a diverse and prosperous company aiming to give your employees a purpose and make a difference in this world.

Harassment is an unwelcome act directed towards another person or group of people based on gender, race, colour, religion, origin, age, disability or sexual orientation. It becomes unlawful when the harassment creates an intimidating, hostile or abusive environment for the victim(s). Sexual harassment is a special type of harassment with sexual advances, remarks and verbal or physical harassment of a sexual nature.

Discrimination is the differential treatment of an individual or group of people based on their race, colour, national origin, religion, sex (including pregnancy and gender identity), age, marital and parental status, disability, sexual orientation, or genetic information.

Ideally you don't want to find yourself in the scenario of the introduction to this book, but the reality is that it may happen in your company at one point or the other. We want to ensure that you are prepared. And if it happens, don't panic – just deal with it.

Pushing the topic aside helps no-one. Remember there are always options.

As a leader and as a company you want to create a place that is effective and equal for everyone.

In these instances when your fundamental company values have been misrepresented due to the action of a person, or several people, it makes sense to send a message to the whole company, that certain behaviours are unacceptable and of consequence.

It may initially cause rumours, or fear amongst the team, but the thought that the teams are protected at a greater level will be more prominent.

You can do this for example in your bi-weekly, or monthly or quarterly 'all company' meetings in person, especially if the team is small still, and particularly when the person who you need to let go sits within the leadership team. Act fast and explain to your employees how they should interact with the press, supposing that the departure will be of interest to external sources. Typically, that should happen at management level.

Top Tips:

- As part of your essential policies build in an anti-harassment and discrimination policy into your code of conduct and share it with each employee.

- Speak about these topics either as part of onboarding process, or on a frequent basis during company meetings; don't shy away.

- When it happens consult with your HR/People team and an external lawyer who is versed in this subject for the country you are operating in. Treat people with respect, as you would like to be treated and keep things confidential.

3.5 – Scaling – As You Grow

Employee Retention

When you think about your company and its health it really comes down to your people and their productivity.

A moderate level of staff turnover can be good for a business; it means fresh ideas and approaches coming in. However, ignoring high levels of employee turnover can be very costly. It will affect and lower internal morale and it could harm the company's reputation and cost you productivity.

If you encourage your employees to provide honest feedback and solutions, you are already off to a good start. Send regular Company Surveys every month or so, as well as specific surveys for example on company culture and health of the company, or manager surveys which should be consistently done every six or twelve months.

As a startup founder, you might think that you don't need to do this because you are in daily contact with your small team and everybody knows everyone else. But if you think about it, that closeness can make it even more difficult for people to say what they really think. It's much more likely that they'll share any concerns or things they are becoming dissatisfied with, or see as a problem about to happen, before the situation gets serious for them and they consider leaving. When your team don't have to tell you face-to-face, they are more likely to share their thoughts, and they will feel they can bring their concerns to your attention, because you've openly asked to hear what they are.

Your survey questions should remain the same each time you survey the team, so that you can create relevant data points to understand the health of your company through different stages.

There are companies who can help you to manage these

programmes and necessary related surveys such as Huler, Peakon, Ellomi, Culture amp, Hibob, Builtforteams, Sapling etc. There are lots of free survey platforms too if your questions are simple and there aren't too many of them. You don't need to go crazy, just asking between three and six simple questions is better than asking none at all!

If your culture encourages learning and that failing is acceptable then you can share the outcome of these surveys at a high level, and if there is something that needs to change, tell the team how the company is going to manage it.

There are other things you can do on employee engagement and retention too. Continuous learning is important for many of us, we want to know and learn as humans. And, as a result, you could offer annual learning benefits, so, for example, you could allocate a set amount per person to use for their personal studies.

You can create, or buy into, an online learning platform so that people can learn new skills in their own time. You may already need an online learning platform as some courses will be mandatory, such as health and safety for example. Coaching and personal development are not just important but can be a high priority for the people who seek to learn and grow in all aspects of their life.

You can run annual charitable incentives where your teams can volunteer time from their working hours. Let's say for example twenty hours per annum that they can spend at the charity of their choice. Or you could ask your employees to donate to a specific company and choose charities which you will match.

Annual company bonuses are good forms of retention as well as continued share and/or restricted stock allocations. Every year you could create a performance review and people could choose maybe between a salary increase, shares or a mix of both, but only if the person's performance and the company performance is positive.

You could provide long standing performance awards or

prizes for those who stay five years and another at ten years and so on, either increasing annual paid holiday, or maybe tech gadgets – you name it. Just check with your HR/People and Legal department what sort of impact that has on the back of the company. Some of these are taxable benefits, some are not. This goes back to knowing and understanding your business plan, and company expenses.

We know you can't do it all in the early days, but as you grow, you are going to need to find ways of keeping your best people. But nothing beats meaningful work and career opportunities, so you must ensure you can provide them.

Offboarding

Don't forget, your employees current, or past are – and remain your brand ambassadors.

We have all heard one story or another where a disgruntled former employee spreads information through their network via social media or the newspaper about their termination from the company that they worked for, and how they have been treated from their point of view, along with their indignant feelings and beliefs of mistreatment. Let's face it, it's not great PR. Most importantly it's potentially disastrous when replacing them and can make life difficult and embarrassing for the great people that still work for you.

So how do you mitigate the risk of that happening to you? The answer is to have a great offboarding experience.

Offboarding is the strategic process of releasing a team member from their contract, either because they have resigned or because you have had to let them go. The process consists of exit interviews, the return of any hardware or software that belongs to the company, creating and filing mandatory forms and documents, as well as ensuring that knowledge and expertise stay within the company and that there is a proper handover to a successor. Please see an example on page 260.

Having a proper process in place, makes people feel valued and appreciated and strengthens your relationship with them. It simply shows professionalism.

Why should you have an offboarding process at all?

If your people feel appreciated, even when they leave, they are more likely to share and pass on their knowledge and expertise before they go. Departing team members are an authentic source of feedback, that you can only get when you offer them the opportunity to share it. When they do, it's helpful if you really listen and care about what they have to say!

There is a chance these people might become your future customers or even team members again one day. They will be of real value to you because they know how your company 'ticks' already and come back with a lot of more experience than they had when they left. It's not unusual for people to be tempted by something that looks like a better offer, only to find that they hate their new job. People go back to their former companies more often that you might think. So, if someone is leaving you whom you are sorry to lose, a good offboarding process leaves the door open if they regret their decision to leave. For people you have let go because of issues at work, then you probably don't want them back, but you do want to minimise the risk of fall out after their departure. Either way, it's a good idea to get things right.

So, what does a good offboarding process look like?

First of all, make time for the employee who is about to exit to ensure they have all the necessary HR related documents such as reference letters, termination letters etc. Apart from the mandatory formal HR meeting, schedule a casual 1-on-1 meeting with them to hear them out as a manager or CEO if your company is small.

If they leave of their own accord, listen and understand why they are leaving. Ask for their honest feedback, concerns, suggestions, ideas on how to make things better in the future. Extend them your help for their transition and remain professional and respectful. At this point, don't validate their feelings and thoughts, give advice or agree to any changes. Listen, thank them for their feedback and wish them well for the future.

Next thing you need to do as a manager or CEO, is communicate the change to everyone who is affected by it, such as their closest team members or those who work closely with them outside of their direct team.

Depending on the reasons for the parting, your communication can include information like the date and reason for leaving, who will be the successor and other details like voluntary actions and supporting measures from your side.

Create some kind of alumni circle, in which former employees receive dedicated newsletters, get invited to special alumni events, where they can network even for their current jobs and receive branded goodies occasionally. If you are planning to scale up quickly, then it's a wise move because finding enough good people is likely to be one of your biggest challenges. Some companies invest a lot in resources, others haven't even thought about it as a useful strategy. But it can pay off handsomely by creating brand ambassadors, valuable word of mouth marketing and creating a network of potential leaders and decision makers in different fields and companies that you might want to collaborate with in the future. Not to forget, it strengthens the culture inside your company at the same time. There is a handy one page offboarding checklist in the back of this book on page 261 which you can copy and use for your Offboardings.

Your People Wrap Up

- **Leadership.** Always work on and demonstrate your Leadership skills.

- **Growth Mindset.** Operate from a growth mindset and facilitate structures to allow your team to do the same.

- **Simple is best.** Think simple when it comes to processes.

- **Longevity.** Longevity is part of business.

- **Consistency.** Always step up your employee experience, never rest.

- **Values.** Operate from your values, even when it gets hard.

COMMUNICATION

Focus your team on your company's goals through effective communication.

4.1. What and Why

Are you Communicating?

Everyone can communicate – can't they?

We all communicate every day, so why do you need to think about internal communication at all? Doesn't it take care of itself?

The answer is no – it doesn't.

It happens, just not the way you want it to.

Without doing things deliberately, things can quickly go off the rails.

If you are going to foster that company culture you have pictured in your mind, if you want people to adopt *The Way We Do Things Around Here* without constantly enforcing rules and behaving like a disciplinarian, then you need to communicate clearly and with intent. When it's done well, it *looks* like it's just happened by accident. Good communication is *almost* invisible at times.

Communication is such a fundamental thing. We all do it, and we all take it for granted. But in professional life, there are different challenges. You want to avoid miscommunication, misinterpretation, speculation and mistrust amongst the team.

The complexity of information flow and provision, the different types of communication available to us, the various channels, the nature of your content and the makeup of the message itself, gives you so many variables that misunderstanding is only a heartbeat away. And what's not said can cause as many problems as saying the wrong thing. It's a minefield for any leader; that's why we are going to spend some time on it here.

Because communication happens everywhere and all the time, your official corporate communication needs to be professional, recognisable and unambiguous. Your unofficial communication is less visible but just as powerful. It is like body language – it's not just the words, it is how it is delivered. How you communicate with your team has the power to inspire, motivate and enthuse people. It also has the power to unwittingly undermine your culture, de-motivate your team, destroy personal trust and crush people's ideas.

We are sure that you don't want to do any of those last things. If you want to be an effective and positively influential founder, read on to find out how to get it right.

Internal Communication

———————— **What is internal communication?** ————————

'Communication – It's a big construct that can mean a lot of things.

Founders need to ensure that people are connected within their company. They need to have open communication both ways, early on and stick with it. It's vital that your people are on the same page and understand the future vision, goals and deadlines.' – Arnnon Geshuri

Internal communication is the essential tool that you have, to shape and nurture your company culture. When you ask people what communication inside a company consists of, you'll often hear the standard responses; emails, press releases, rousing talks to the team and social media postings. But it's so much more than that.

Communication includes anything from a subconscious hand gesture to an email sent a day later; to *not* responding to a question, and yes, that big speech in your team meeting.

Communication can be any verbal or non-verbal message in the widest sense and will be interpreted by the recipient, intended or not. We communicate, even when we don't intend to.

Austrian psychologist and communication scientist Paul Watzlawick points out that "*One cannot not communicate*".

At a later stage in most companies, you will probably need a clearly thought out communication strategy that's delivered through your internal communication plan. But in the early days, it's unlikely that you'll have time for much in the way of formal processes – but you do need to communicate with intent and with clear goals in mind.

Internal communication is – and will always remain – the responsibility of the top management and the leadership, which makes it your responsibility. In the future you would be well advised to hire someone to take care of it full time, but that person can only prepare it *for you* to deliver it or at least back it up with your behaviour and deeds. So, get used to this part of your job – because that's what communication is: your job.

Things go wrong really quickly if you aren't on top on what's being communicated as well as what's not being said, and a great deal of damage can be done without realising it. By the time you see the harm that's been done, it's often too late.

I think the description that Bettina Andresen Guimarães gives of how important it is within the context of a startup or early-stage business is a great starting point.

'If you don't communicate actively, people will have their own ideas of what you want to achieve and what you want them to do, so they will fabricate their own interpretation. Only by being direct and explicit will you achieve clarity in communication and be able to unite people towards a common goal.'

Without some basics in place, your team will inevitably start using their own tools and systems. They will communicate and collaborate in ways they picked up from previous companies using what methods and channels are the most convenient for them. Once habits get established, they spread quickly. By then, it's extremely hard to establish common ways of communicating and collaborating and the last thing you want is to find yourself having to force everyone to use the same tools in the same way when they have got used to doing it in a way that suits each of them individually. For example, streamlining everyone into using a common naming convention and folder structure in one single data management tool becomes a change management project that distracts people from their core tasks.

It's much easier to put in place solid communication culture right from the start than to battle headwinds and resistance from your team, who will be forced to change their established behaviour.

Top Tip:

To keep it simple there should be a top level folder for each division or functional unit (e.g. IT, HR, Marketing, Finance etc.) and in each one the project folders such as projects, clients, finances, admin and so on. Within those project folders will be subfolders helping you with the status of these documents like planned, in progress, final, archive. Use the actual date at the end of each document's name.

```
▼ 📁 MARKETING
    ▼ 📁 ADMIN
        ▶ 📁 IN PROGRESS
        ▶ 📁 FINAL
        ▶ 📁 ARCHIVE
    ▶ 📁 CLIENTS
    ▶ 📁 FINANCES
    ▶ 📁 PROJECTS
```

Depending on the nature and industry of your business, there are the following **central functional units** which you will need in the beginning:

- Management
- IT
- Research and Development
- Marketing and Sales
- Human Resources
- Customer Service
- Accounting and Finance
- Purchase

Of course, it varies according to your liking, requirements and nature of your business. For example, Communication (internal and external) most likely will sit under Marketing in the beginning and maybe you don't need sales yet. You might not even need IT in the very early stages, because you as a team can manage with a few programs and if you have technical problems, you might be fine with the customer support of those programs.

Don't forget to establish a legal unit mid-term, but in the beginning you might be fine with external resources here. Same goes for finance. Maybe your HR department/person can take care of the wage payment and you can use external tax consultants for the rest.

And when it comes to purchase, well, we've seen it working that almost the whole team had access to a budget and could make purchases with the company's money as long as given rules were complied, such as not more than a certain amount, everything above that amount needed an informal written approval by the CEO and it had to be added to a simple excel spreadsheet, who purchased what, where, what for and at what cost.

Introduce simple rules with the folder structure, such as your one and only naming convention, a rule for how to use your structure, what goes where, and rules like:

- Don't save documents on your desktop.

- Limit folder creation. When you're creating folders, think minimal. Most files can fit somewhere in your hierarchy if you've done a good job of initially mapping it out. In general, only create new folders if you find yourself repeatedly coming back to save similar files in the same place, only to find that it doesn't exist yet.

- Apply a one and only naming convention.

- Get file synch up and running, so everyone has access to the latest version of your files and documents.

The four goals of internal communication

Everything will become clear and simple once you know that everything you do needs to be rooted in the four goals of internal communication which are to keep people:

Aligned
Informed
Connected
Motivated

Communication for Everyone

To discuss this topic adequately would go beyond the scope of this book, but we don't want to leave it unmentioned either. And we would like to give you a short piece of advice. When thinking about communication, take a few moments and actively reflect on how your team is made up. Is it straightforward or is it an atypical mix of people? We talked about different cultures in the Culture chapter already – remember that culture also includes age, gender, race, religion, upbringing, sexual orientation, handicaps and so on.

Your team is your unique target group after all. Consider them your internal customers, who need to buy in to your requirements and ideas, thus into what you communicate. So, it's worth being doubly aware that if you've got an atypical mix of people that you'll have to invest harder in effective communications. We would like to draw your attention to asking yourself things like:

Is my team from several different geographical cultures that typically work differently in the workplace?

Does my team have a gender imbalance that affects how we might communicate?[3]

Is there an inherent challenge because we have 80% remote software engineers versus 20% in house marketers?

Are there huge age gaps within departments, which create lots of target groups when it comes to preferred channels?

How can I encourage an open, non-biased and non-prejudiced communication culture within my team and how do I avoid any pitfalls myself when communicating?

All those factors, amongst others, will mean you need to change your style of communicating, dependent on the audience. The following reference may help you.

(from 'The Culture Map' by Erin Meyer):

- ▦ **Communicating:** explicit vs. implicit.
- ▦ **Evaluating:** direct negative feedback vs. indirect negative feedback.
- ▦ **Persuading:** deductive vs. inductive.
- ▦ **Leading:** egalitarian vs. hierarchical.
- ▦ **Deciding:** consensual vs. top down.
- ▦ **Trusting:** task vs. relationship.
- ▦ **Disagreeing:** confrontational vs. avoid confrontation.
- ▦ **Scheduling:** structured vs. flexible.

According to Meyer, people from different cultures fall on these scales differently and thus, interaction between people from different cultures will be easier if they consider where they are located on these scales in relation to each other. For example, the Dutch are very direct when it comes to evaluating and will most likely sound rude and insulting to a Japanese, where negative feedback is given very discreetly.

But at this point it is enough for you to be aware of the existence of diversity in people, their preferences and requirements, and that it affects your communication.

Hybrid or Fully Remote Workplace

How do you manage communication in a hybrid or even a fully remote workplace? You might be relieved to hear, that many of the communication rules are the same as for fully onsite teams. In fact, the basics, such as being clear, brief, unambiguous, timely, professional, mindful of cultural differences, and so on, never change. But there are nuances to the delivery of your communication when it comes to where people work.

An in person all hands meeting cannot happen if half of the team is not physically there. You need to make sure that it is being streamed to remote working people, who should be able to participate with the same duties and rights as the people on site such as being able to ask questions, chat with other participants, be seen and be punctual. Remote working people are also missing out on the social aspect, when sitting in front of a screen all day. So, you need to focus more on the team based communication by making sure 'water cooler' conversations are still facilitated. You can do this easily by providing an open social chat channel on Slack.

With people working remotely, your internal communication needs to focus more on people's mental health and help people feel they belong, which usually happens automatically when people meet, collaborate and socialise in person. This is tricky to maintain when your team is working remotely, but even harder when half are remote and half are not, because this might cause cliques excluding those not physically present. They miss out on the social life, which happens in an office, and which simply does not exist with fully remote teams where everyone is on the same page social-wise.

Furthermore, how can you, as the founder, or any of your leaders show presence and be 'seen', when you're physically not there. It's one thing to casually walk up to you in the canteen but a completely different matter to actively call you or write you a message. You inevitably become untouchable and unapproachable as you are not present. As a result, your role model function, your passion and everything you as the founder stand for becomes invisible.

If you're wondering what you can do about it, here are a few ideas:

- Offer to hold an AMA (ask me anything) session regularly,

which is blocked in your calendar and where you answer anyone's questions in a dedicated open chat channel (just be mindful of confidentiality).

- Organise a 'founder's couch' every month, which is basically an open meeting all can attend, where people can see you, raise their hands and ask you questions or talk to you about anything. We have even seen startups with bigger teams doing that with a certain topic prepared each time. Everyone could vote on beforehand, like our investor relations, the plans for our prototypes, funding plans, gender imbalance in recruiting, etc. (again, confidentiality needs to be priority).

- Establish fun company traditions and quirks like company-internal (funny) backgrounds for calls, team fitness challenges, the joke/trivia/quote of the day on a certain channel, a virtual book club and so on.

- Host casual chat channels like #foodies, #catlovers, #parentaltips, #fitnesschallenge, #gardeningtips, #good-reads etc.

- Last but by no means least, organise virtual team meetings, happy hours and parties. You could, for example, send a box with a branded towel and a branded frisbee to every team member's home before the day of the virtual summer party and have everyone order takeaway for a fixed amount of money, which you can endorse afterwards. The party itself could consist of a summer feeling contest, a fun quiz about your company or different cultures (which would raise awareness for this topic once more in a fun way), a DJ for everyone to dance to and of course everything else you would normally do from a stage, like your CEO speech, fun awards, a virtual interactive magic show, the company band playing live or whatever your parties are usually like.

Rapport Talk versus Report Talk

Like it or not, communication is everywhere and it happens all the time. Just think of the last time you walked into a room and felt ignored, which can only happen if someone doesn't communicate with you. How did that make you feel? We are hardwired to notice these things and some people are more sensitive to every little nuance of communication than others. Every gesture you make, every smile, every missing gesture, every email, every time you walk in a room or hit send on your phone or keyboard – you are communicating.

So, it's a good idea to do it well and become more and more self-aware as your leadership style develops.

Something else to be aware of is your own personal communication style. Each of us tends to gravitate towards one of two extremes. We call them rapport talk and report talk. People who are rapport orientated generally aim to build rapport before they deliver the message or they deliver the message with very 'soft edges'. People who are report orientated get straight to the point, don't see any need for more words than is necessary to deliver the message. Which one are you?

The challenges come when people with the two different styles communicate. The report talk person takes pride in getting straight to the point. The rapport talk person wonders what they've done wrong when the message has been delivered so bluntly.

Let's look at a quick example. A rapport talk person is likely to open a conversation, or email, on a Monday by opening with 'I hope you had a great weekend', and the report talk person ignores it and goes straight in with the response 'Have you sent the sales figures through?' When that little bit of communication friction happens frequently, it can lead to people feeling that they don't know how they should communicate with you.

The reverse can happen too, the report talk person asks a direct question, the rapport talk person wants to make sure the atmosphere is positive before they respond, so they take a few moments to build rapport. The report talk person wonders if they'll ever get to the point and starts to get a little irritated.

It's not hard to see how easily people can get offended or how people can think others are wasting valuable time on chitchat instead of getting to the point!

It can be helpful to share that little insight with your team as then, if you are under pressure and report talk has to take over, they don't get offended by your directness. Or if it's just your personal style, tell them so they don't get offended. If you are a rapport talk person, make sure your message can be easily heard and doesn't get lost in the niceties.

It can be very noticeable when you observe people interacting and in meetings, just how this small difference in communication styles can lead to untold amounts of friction between team members. Sophisticated leaders know when to consciously zone into either of the two styles, whatever their personal preferences are. You can too. It just takes a little practice. It will give you the ability to not take things too personally if you have extreme report talkers that you do business with who communicate in a very direct way. It's just their style. And have a little patience with the rapport talkers, just help them to stick to the point and not get distracted.

But you know about it now, so you're ready for it and can use your new found knowledge to good effect to keep relationships on a solid footing.

YOU Set The Tone

You really need people to be problem solvers. After all, startups are all about solving problems. Some days you will feel like there are nothing but problems! But when your team is communicating in an open and healthy way they will amaze you with their ambition, thoughts and ideas.

They need to feel they can communicate that.

And they need to feel that people are listening.

--------------------- **Project Manager's story** ---------------------

One day, in an early stage startup during a townhall meeting, just when the Q&A section was about to start, a project manager stood up and asked if he could say a few words. He walked to the front of the 40+ people and you could see he was shaking with excitement. He was about to do something which involuntarily shaped the way the whole team communicated from that moment on.

He said 'I've made a mistake and it costs us 15,000€ of extra supplies and two weeks of our time.' At that moment, you could hear a pin drop. For such a young startup, that was an awful lot of money and every delayed day meant a threat to the very existence of the company, so what he had just said shook everyone to the bone. He explained shortly what he had done wrong and why it had such a severe impact. Worst thing was that it was an avoidable mistake. He ended his speech with 'When I told Jan and Niklas (his managers and founders) I was prepared to be fired. Instead, they listened carefully and quietly, asked questions to understand the full scope. And then they said, that it's a lesson learned and we have to establish processes and check lists for certain things now. They made me the VP of processes.' Everyone in the room giggled with relief.

'Also, they will have to bring forward the next funding

round now, thus have shifted their focus on that, which is a good delegation exercise for them. As for the extra work I have caused you all, I sincerely apologize and hope we can all learn from my mistake.'

Everyone stood up, applauded and from that moment on, the team dared to challenge the status quo, share ideas for yet missing rules, and – most importantly – speak up about anything that was open, honest and self-reflective. It was a communication and error-culture established in the natural way as a result of the founders acting professionally, prudently and empathetically.

Inside Out!

Communicate from the Inside Out. So, what does this mean?

It simply means you should always communicate internally before you communicate externally.

How would you feel if somewhere that you worked had something really important happening, and you only found out about it from the media or from somebody outside the business?

I'm sure you can think of a news story where team members discovered that the company was closing, expanding, under new ownership or some other major news by hearing it through the grapevine, via social media, or from a newspaper or TV. That's a shocking example of a total lack of effective internal communications. It's hugely damaging to the reputations of both companies and individual leaders. If you want your people to feel valued and included, always communicate inside the company first before you ever communicate outwards.

It doesn't have to be a week before the big news hits the media, because you cannot risk them talking to media beforehand.

There's always a balance to strike, just don't leave things to chance.

When you communicate regularly you eliminate the risk of speculation and miscommunication too.

There's nothing worse than gossip for distracting people and sowing a climate of fear. No one works well in that environment. There will always be confidential things you can't tell everyone, especially as you grow, so be transparent about that as well. People understand as long as they are told that there are some things you cannot share.

For example, if you are in discussions about funding and can't share it yet, if people are worried about their jobs or their projects, it might help to let them know something is happening without sharing the details. You could say, 'We are in discussion with an investor, I can't tell you names or numbers, but we are in talks, nothing is signed yet, but you will be the first ones to know'.

Try to be as transparent as you can, as open as you can, and as fair as you can.

If people feel informed and know that you will consider them first, they will feel valued.

Be clear about your role so people understand that you won't be sharing everything.

A good way to do this is by telling people something along the lines of, 'Look folks, everybody has different responsibilities here and my role as CEO / Founder gives me the responsibility to make sure you all have a job and that the company thrives. There are things which might be interesting, but not relevant, and I don't want to flood you with information. If I did that you would most likely start having to decide what's important, what's relevant and what's management noise. I'll do my best to make sure you know everything you need to know that's relevant for your work. But do come and ask me if you hear something over the watercooler that bothers you. Approach me directly before you speculate and ask me about it.

But just know there are some things which we cannot share with you, and other things you probably cannot share with us on a regular basis. That's fine, as long as you know that my door is always open.'

Choose your own words. What's important here is the wider principles; people need to know you will tell them first, keep them informed; you will tell the internal team before the outside world is talking about the future of the company and that you will answer questions. Put simply, you will keep the lines open and expect other people to do the same.

What is Good Communication?

What does a good communication culture look like?

Simply put good communication is:

- active listening and asking questions
- adapting your communication style and channels where appropriate
- fair negotiation
- an open and honest information flow
- sending clear and concise messages
- giving/receiving feedback professionally.

You know good communication is happening when:

- Your team members have made a habit of discussing business matters with each other and with you.
- People dare to challenge ideas and ask questions.

- Your team members ask questions about a message you sent out.
- People talk about private things and share personal stories with each other.
- People try to solve conflicts professionally.
- They ask for each other's opinions or help.
- They give and take feedback regularly.
- People search for and share knowledge.
- People use your channels for communication and collaboration.
- They focus on the topic at hand and don't get personal.
- They listen to what you have to say and translate it into their behaviour or change their behaviour accordingly.
- When your analytics or observations show that most of your team received your message.

Mind your words

... As they shape the way we perceive our world.

Anthropologist and linguist Edward Sapir and his student Benjamin Whorf created the Sapir-Whorf hypothesis, which states that our understanding and perception of the world depends largely on our thought processes, and these again are limited by our language. That means the culture you live in creates the need for certain words and shapes the way we perceive the world.

You might have heard about NLP (Neuro Linguistic Programming) which claims that you can change your thought patterns and behaviour through language and with that you can achieve any goal in your life.

By the way you frame something and how you talk, which words and phrases you choose, you are cuing others to think about it in a specific way.

For example, a sexist language influences the way our society views men and women. The first picture which comes to mind when talking about a 'policeman' is a man and for 'nurse' it's a woman, isn't it? Well, there you go then.

What has this to do with your company?

As you can see, language is an important asset in shaping your company culture. So, use your company communication for your cause by choosing the right language. 'Onboarding experience' sounds way more human-centric than 'onboarding process', doesn't it? Same for 'People Department' versus 'Human Resources'.

Ever thought why bigger companies call their meeting rooms after big cities, where you'd want to go to on a city trip? Or why Google chose TGIF (Thank God It's Friday) for their weekly meeting?

Just let this resonate with you for a while and think again if you want to call your team 'employees' or rather 'team mates', 'colleagues', or 'cultural co-founders' in your communication.

4.2 How to Set It up

Choose your Channels

Which channels do you need in the beginning? All the tools, processes and structures will grow with your company as you need them. In the early days you will more likely be successful if you don't overcomplicate things.

The basics you need to think about in the early days are simple.

Here is a little secret I want to unwrap for you. Remember the four goals of communication which are Align, Inform, Connect and Motivate? If you can reach all those goals with your channels, you're all set up.

——————————— Goal 1: Align people ———————————

We talked about ways to communicate your culture in the first chapter of this book, so I won't repeat it here. But in case you need an example of how 'pinning a channel to each goal' works, let me explain swiftly.

You can align your people to your culture via all the channels such as your all hands meeting, your intranet, instant messaging tool, branded pens, stickers, socks, laptop webcam covers, t-shirts, peppermint boxes and so on.

Additionally, aligning people means they have to be on the same page for *How You Do Things Around Here*, so they must have access to the cultural documents. You need to store them in a safe and official place that everyone can access, easily. I'm talking about an *Intranet* or a *Document Management System (DMS) like Drive, Dropbox, DocuWare, Sharepoint...*

Goal 2: Inform people

To keep your people informed about everything relevant you need a place where all the information is stored that's key to the business. An Intranet and DMS also serve well for this purpose. To keep the actual information flow running, you'll need channels, where you can 'push' information actively, such as the regular all-hands meeting, emails, instant messaging tools, like Slack, Teams or WhatsApp or others.

Goal 3: Connect people

Connecting people needs to happen on two levels; collaboratively and socially.

For a *collaborative* connectivity among your team, you need to think of channels like project management tools such as *Asana*, *Citrix*, *Jira*, *Trello* and DMS again.

For social interaction you can offer meetings, an instant messaging tool, team-events like evenings-out or team-lunches. And here again, you, yourself are a role model and that is a channel in itself. Use your tools, adhere to your rules, stay connected, socialise and take an interest in your people.

Goal 4: Motivate people

Feeling well informed, being aligned with your culture and being connected are already motivating. But don´t neglect the active part in motivating your people by celebrating achievements, showing your passion, giving a motivational speech, a Well done or a Thank you, but also by facilitating and participating in any social event. **AND WALK AROUND YOUR TEAM AND TALK TO THEM!**

So, here is my idea for an initial internal communication infrastructure:

- a weekly all hands meeting for the personal touch
- a mail program (e.g. Google Mail)
- an instant messaging tool (e.g. Slack)
- a DMS (e.g. Dropbox Business)
- a project management tool, if not already incorporated in your DMS (e.g. Trello)
- plus events, parties and maybe some offline channels like branded clothing, lanyards, keyrings, cardholders, reusable cups, wall-tattoos etc.

It makes sense to do some research to find out what is out there and compare functionalities, costs, confidentiality regulations (if applicable) and support or service. Also, don't hesitate to ask around for recommendations. Ask your team if they can recommend any tool and why. Have them provide a list of pros and cons and all the information you need in order to make an educated and fact-based decision. Also ask your broader network, other founders, your investors anyone with an interest in the company. Don't be shy in asking for help implementing the tools and supporting your team with the initial steps with a manual or a quick training on how to use it, maybe during one of your regular team meetings.

Make sure you know how to work with the tools yourself and get familiar with them, so that you can be the driving force behind the adoption of it and a role model for them which will help to reinforce their usage. If you don't make it clear that this is the way forward, you will find people using their personal tools of choice which will mean that information will very quickly get out of control and be stuffed away in the dark corners of various apps and tools. So, make the decision as you can always change your mind later as your needs change, write it down, inform the team and make sure they know how to use what's been selected.

But most importantly you must follow the same rules yourself! Exclusively and ruthlessly!

Remember that culture is simply *The Way We Do Things Around Here* and people are looking to you for guidance. Your culture starts with the way **YOU** do things around here.

Set the Ground Rules

Since Netflix CEO Reed Hastings introduced a 'no rules' culture at Netflix and wrote a book about it along with business professor Erin Meyer, scientific interest has increased, and other companies have tried to copy their approach.

Of course, you can draw inspiration from it and keep rules in your company to a minimum. But experience has shown, that in the chaotic and turbulent times of a young startup, you definitely need some rules in order to get some structure and order in the way your team works. If you think using the word **RULES** will put people off, think of another word to encompass *The Way We Do Things Around Here*, or something that you come up with yourself.

Believe me, you will know when it is time to introduce a rule for something. When you do, write it down, store it in a central place where everyone can review it at any time and communicate it to your team officially. The collection of rules will grow with you and they will need to be adjusted as you go. This way they are there without too much effort and on demand. However, only keep the essential ones to help with your development at any given time.

Role Model and Reinforce

Communicate
　　　Communicate
　　　　　　Communicate

Do it regularly and be consistent.

You need to use your agreed tools and channels and no others, which comply with your rules and processes without exception, and which live up to your communication culture.

You have set up the tool landscape and how to use it, now show them exactly what it means. You always need to be aware of your responsibility as a role model.

This holds especially true for the communication culture. If you don't look left and right before crossing the street, how can you expect your kids to do it?

As a founder, you know your team aren't kids, but the same principles apply. Your team members will automatically look to you and copy your behaviours. Sometimes they do it unconsciously, and sometimes they are well aware of looking at the leader for guidance on *How We Do Things Around Here*. People will see behaviours from you which sends a signal, 'If she does that, it must be OK for me to do the same,' even if you don't realise it!

'People and communication skills, knowing and understanding other people, including yourself and learning to communicate appropriately with them are the top essential skills founders need to have, in order to succeed.' – Bettina Andresen Guimarães (Authentic Wow)

It sounds easier than it really is, because we all have days when we are exhausted and don't care about the small things like switching on the dishwasher or neglecting some little rules around the place for example – if you finish the toilet paper, then replace it.

These are the days when we feel we simply don't have the energy to suppress bad habits such as hiding in your office, communicating poorly or not at all, because you just don't feel like talking in front of your team right now.

But here comes the unadorned truth. It is your job to have energy for that!

How can you expect your team to be good at their jobs, if you are not fully invested in yours?

I've known people who hang up a visible reminder in their personal workspace to make sure they remember. You could have a screensaver or carry something with you which says exactly that: 'IT IS YOUR **JOB** TO HAVE ENERGY FOR EVERYTHING.'

Whatever works for you, do it!

If it would help to ask for feedback on your communication skills from your leadership team regularly, then ask them!

Maybe you prefer taking on a communication coach and working on your skills actively and professionally? Then find one!

No matter how you overcome the bad communication habits or days, when you just don't feel like it, just do it!

How you want people to feel, behave, communicate and collaborate starts with you. As we said before, internal communication does not get solved by hiring a communication expert, nor does it stop being the responsibility of the leader.

It is important you always have **your** sh*t together. You must know what and how you want to do something and most importantly, you need to do it – especially when it comes to communicating, as you now know. This is your job as a founder and as a leader. Let's have a look at this job of yours in detail.

TAKE CARE OF YOURSELF.
You need me-time to keep it all together and you must plan ahead and work on the founder role you want to fill. You also want your team to remain healthy and sustainable, and you as a role model can show them how they should, and can, take care of themselves.

BE ALIGNED WITH YOUR CO-FOUNDERS.
If mummy said no, maybe daddy will say yes. Children learn

quickly to play parents against each other to get what they want. Again, we're not saying your team members are like children, but you as founders definitely do need to apply the number one parenting rule. Always follow the same line and don't contradict each other. You are the Alpha-team who need to stick together and form a solid united front. Be loyal, integrated and communicate with each other – always.

BE AND REMAIN AUTHENTIC.

If you feel your personality is hindering you, for example, you've always been the clown and you fear that people will not take you seriously, get a coach! You can be true to yourself and at the same time be professional at work by adhering to rules or principles you set up for yourself. It's not changing who you are, it's growing into your role of who you want to be professionally.

Stay informed yourself. Introduce direct report meetings, in which you meet those in your teams who report directly to you. Ideally, this should be a weekly face to face meeting. Let them update you with a fixed agenda consisting of:

How they are in general.

Are there any issues including private ones (if they want to share) which might influence their job?

What have they accomplished in the week?

What are they planning for the week ahead?

Is help required from you, other teams or external resources?

Create a priority list together and see if it changes from week to week.

Agree with them to do the same with their direct reports.

BE APPROACHABLE AND REMAIN AVAILABLE.

You are serving your team by providing them a purpose, a vision, a goal and not to forget, food on the table and a job to do. Don't close the door unless it's absolutely necessary. Actively invite people to approach you. Approach them yourself. Show them how close they can be with you. Go for walks with your early team members and talk about private stuff. Take an interest in them.

BE FAIR AND HONEST.

This can be challenging, even brutal at times, especially when the first employee you have to let go is an old friend of yours. But it is far more important for your company to thrive and your culture to develop in the right direction. By always being fair and honest, you will either keep that person as a friend or lose someone who never really was one. It is essential that you set rules and principles that you follow rigorously and without exception, and make it known to the team.

BE TRANSPARENT AND OPEN.

This should reflect in your internal communication strategy. Share the good news and the bad. Treat your team with respect and candour even if you cannot share all the details. You must be open and honest about the facts. Always communicate internally before externally without exception! There is no bigger breach of trust between team members and an employer than when they learn something relevant about their company through external sources first.

ESTABLISH AN ERROR AND FEEDBACK CULTURE.

Errors are only human and will inevitably happen. By hiding them, no one will learn from them. Even worse, it might even lead to catastrophic consequences. Make sure to communicate openly about mistakes and encourage team members to admit their own by establishing a culture in which *It's OK To Make Mistakes Around Here* just as long as lessons are learned from it. This goes hand in hand with having a strong feedback culture. Your team members should feel confident and safe enough not only to admit mistakes, but also to challenge you and give you honest feedback.

> *If you have open and fluid communication, it will drive innovation and connectivity. I have seen companies succeed because they encourage debate and voicing of opposing opinions and they celebrate differences and create courageous conversations. Don't just hire people to say yes to everything you want but get people on board who professionally challenge you. It will make your product and company better.*
> Arnnon Geshuri

Consider (cultural) differences. Even two people from the same country might have different regional subcultures, education or upbringing, backgrounds and personalities. Especially with intercultural differences, there can be different languages and/ or styles of communication, there can be misunderstandings and frustration because of the smallest things. Make your team aware of intercultural differences and sensitise them by addressing this topic openly and regularly.

This will result in a safe space for them all to thrive so make these differences your asset instead of a roadblock. Your company will become fertile ground for creative thinking and problem solving.

Make your message understood and not just heard. Team members are drowning in information but starving for understanding. Make the important interesting and always try to include a what, why, when, how and who in your communication. You will have created a strong internal communication strategy and plan, now you need to follow through your strategy and put your plan into action every day with no exceptions.

Top Tip:

Show confidence. Even if you are insecure or cannot answer all their questions yet, remain calm and confident. Use your body language and speech as a tool of confidence for yourself and your team.[4]

Your team needs you as their tower of strength. Your communication is your route to that. They need you! Careful thinking about what you say and how you say it can make a big difference in how your message is received and how confident people will feel with you as their leader. For example, instead of 'Sorry for the delay' you could say, 'Thank you for your patience. Instead of 'What time would suit you?' you can say 'Would 9:30 work for you? Instead of 'I hope this makes sense' you can say 'Let me know if you have questions. Instead of 'I think maybe we should…' you can say 'It would be best if we did…'. Instead of 'Sorry, my fault! I totally missed that' you could say 'Nice catch! Thank you for letting me know'. You see, words make all the difference.

4.3 Getting Up and Running

Goal 1 – Keep People ALIGNED

Use your internal communications to keep people aligned with the driving force behind your company: your company culture.

If you were to wake your team up in the middle of the night, could they instantly tell you:

- The overall mission of the company
- The company values
- What is expected of them today, this week, this month and this year
- What the rest of the company is doing
- How everyone treats each other

If the answer is no, then you have lots of work to do!

You need to get those messages out loud and clear and expect people to know the answers. These are the questions that bring your culture to life.

Make these questions the bedrock of your own communication. Make the answers be seen, heard, felt and lived.

Be creative about it, involve your whole team. Make it an enjoyable voluntary task to join the culture task force and come up with creative ways to communicate your culture. Create screensavers with the meeting rules, discuss real life stories and let every team member share their explanation of your culture in your team meetings regularly, have (internal) merchandise, such as branded umbrellas, bottle openers or frisbees. Dedicate a whole wall to a makeshift organisational chart, where everyone can pin their picture and a card with their role, responsibilities, skills and interests, until you grow too big and need a tool for that.

Often, I have been asked by colleagues to create an organisation chart per department, where the relationships between teams and departments is shown, thus how each team works with other ones and how they feed into each other. Engage them and make them cultural co-founders.

Indirectly you should communicate your culture as often as you can without sounding dull. It's a fine line between bragging about your cool culture and reminding people in a humble but steady and confident way about what 'living your culture' really means by telling them again and again what you did and why, based on your culture.[5]

You can do this by mentioning the value behind a decision. For example, if one of your values is sustainability, you could announce a new partnership based on your decision: we partnered with company XYZ, because they offered the best approach to a sustainable supply chain.

Goal 2 – Keep People Informed

A great bit of advice to do this simply comes from the CEO of Front, Mathilde Collin. She sends out three different types of email on a regular basis and has a template on her computer that she just fills in depending on which one she wants to send. If you want to be consistent and do the same then just put a diary entry in and make sure you do it on time. Here's what she sends out and the time she expects it to take her:

1. **A weekly CEO email to the whole team every Friday. Content: The Weekly Update**
   It will take you about an hour in the beginning, especially since you need to retrieve the information from the responsible person. But here is a personal tip from me: block twenty minutes in each of those peoples' calendar every Friday morning to send you their updates and numbers

213

proactively by a certain time and create a template for your email, in which you only need to fill in their input and you'll reduce it to fifteen minutes work.

What exactly should be in this email? For example, the current week's revenue, product updates, recruiting numbers, the number of likes and shares on social media, what's on the roadmap for next week or whatever else you want to regularly disseminate around your company.

2. **A weekly CEO email to her direct reports. Sent weekly either on Mondays or Fridays for the next week. Content: Weekly goals**

What are the company goals for this week? What really burns under your nails? What do they have to achieve and how can you help them? Make a priority list if it changes from week to week. For example:

From: CEO
To: All Staff
Re: The Weekly Update

Hi all,

Here is my weekly top-of-mind-list for you:
 – get familiar with our new ....
 – define Q4 goals and focus on team work
 – recruit top talent for engineering, fill team lead position (any referrals?)
 – keep onboarding ....

and here is what I will spend time on:
 – continue preparing next funding round
 – board meeting
 – attending ...... conference

---

3. **A monthly CEO email to your investors. Content: Monthly update**

Inform them about the KPIs, the number of new clients, your revenue, size of the team, key events, both good and bad, plus what you're going to do about it. Of course, you want to please your investors, but keep in mind that investors are usually well informed about what's going on in your industry and in startups in general. They know that there are ups and downs. They appreciate being informed, especially about the negative side of things because this means they will trust you. Plus, you might be surprised about what they are willing and able to help you with. After all, they do have a stake in your success. So, be as transparent as you can, and if the need arises include questions or requests for help in your email. Honesty always wins.

You start to see from experienced CEOs that good communication isn't left to chance. It's a habit and a discipline and it essential for the smooth running of your company. Just sending emails out randomly when you have something to say will soon end up as something that people will only read if it applies to them. Communications get missed, misinterpreted and can end up rambling or giving the wrong information to the wrong people. Mathilde's method of scheduling her communications is an excellent discipline which not only keeps on top of communications but gives her a channel to make sure she knows what's going on in the company all times and what the priorities are.

Goal 3 – Keep People Connected

This can be a challenging balance to strike. You need to give people the tools and opportunities to get together and socialise. It's difficult to balance when you need to let people take longer breaks and talk privately during their work time which will create bonds and friendships while you are the founder, colleague and role model.

You might not feel like engaging in private talk yourself or participating in yet another night out with the team. But it is important. You should see it as a personal investment in your company and communication culture.

You might choose to establish weekly all-hands meetings where you share news and updates about all areas of the company or elaborate on your latest CEO email. This is also the place to address cultural differences, letting people share their stories, fostering your culture and give them the opportunity to ask questions.

To make it a bit more social and to encourage people to attend, you can reveal an interesting 'number of the week such as how many metres of cables are built into our prototype, or, if you prefer, have someone tell the 'joke of the week, or present a riddle at the end of each meeting with a little incentive for the first one to solve it.

You could encourage lunching together each month, think of creative ways to get people to socialise. One team I know used to have 'Thirsty Thursday', where everyone met in town once a month and the first drink was on the company.

What about a TED'sday? TED stands for Technology, Education and Design and are free inspirational talks posted on the internet. Show a TED talk on the big screen in your meeting room and everyone is invited to join and eat their lunch there on a regular day of the week or month. TED talks are great for starting discussions. Choose the talk carefully and you'll end up with a fun, engaging debate that will expand people's horizons and leadership skills. Plus, when your team grows, this is a great opportunity to get to know each other better.

There are many creative and enjoyable ways to enable and encourage your team to socialise. And it's not only fun for them, but also an important tool to keep everyone motivated and productive. It will create stronger bonds between people, which leads to an increase in morale, self-regulation and effective collaboration, since people will start to understand who to ask for which expertise, skill or knowledge – and will more likely dare to walk over to a colleague and ask for help.

Goal 4 – Keep People Motivated

We've talked about aligning people with the mission and values, updating people with business news from you as the CEO, and about connecting the team, but those things are all about the business. Motivation is a much more personal thing. Whereas the business news is very much about the head, motivation is much more about winning hearts.

To win hearts you need to communicate good news. Share the successes of individual team members. Congratulate people in public for a job well done. Praise is a major motivator. Share your excitement and passion for the future. There are lots of ways to do it.

Steve Jobs used to do it from stage to his team announcing the release of new products or the latest innovations that they were working on. You could almost feel the excitement in the room through the camera. But it can be even simpler than that. Just stopping by people's desks and asking how they're doing can make a huge difference to somebody's day. Just smiling at people as you walk through to your desk instead of walking through the office thinking about the next round of funding and not acknowledging your team works wonders. This is something we've probably all done at some point, but it doesn't motivate those people around you.

The Power of Feedback

In theory, a strong feedback culture allows every team member to feel confident to give and receive feedback constructively and professionally from anyone else in the company – regardless of their position.

What this means essentially, is everyone is happy to approach anyone with an observation, an opinion or give a professional critique in a way that initiates a change of behaviour, perspective or thought, which is not offensive to the individual's cultural understanding of good feedback.

Interestingly, most people focus on negative feedback, but it is as essential, if not more so, to give positive feedback to each other too. That motivates and reinforces good behaviour and is a great approach to any task or problem implying that the direct opposite would be wrong and not helpful.

That's the theory – but the reality is that most people don't give good feedback and most of us aren't very good at taking it!

Every team member needs to understand the importance and benefit of giving and receiving feedback and how to do it professionally and constructively. It's up to you to create a safe environment for everyone to express their opinion and make observations. If you resist feedback yourself, you can hardly expect other people to take it well. If your team witness others – especially the leaders – giving and receiving meaningful feedback regularly, in a constructive way, it will become normal and people adapt quickly. So, make your leadership team, especially yourself, model strong feedback principles and ensure that team leaders have regular 1-on-1 meetings with their direct reports and encourage them to ask and share feedback on demand.

And by this I don't only mean your office, your leadership team manners or your culture, but also people's mindset. During the hiring process you should find out whether someone has a growth mindset, which means, they believe their abilities can be developed through dedication and hard work. Those with a growth mindset love to learn and tend to take feedback as an opportunity to improve. Nurture a growth mindset in everyone in your company and if your team members don't know what Growth Mindset is, then show them the TED talk about it!

You can't expect people to just 'know' how to give and take feedback. They need training and a structure to make sure things don't get personal. It's a very specific skill that people are not born with. Most of us need to learn how to do it.

So, set up your company feedback rules, provide feedback training and make it routine for everyone. Consider annual workshops or online training for them – and for yourself if it's not something you are skilled at!

You also need to provide the right tools and opportunities for giving feedback. It can be a sincerely lived 'open door policy', a feedback box in the hallway or a voted trustee within the team, who can help distribute certain types of feedback, which individuals might not want to give personally. Having said that, this anonymous feedback practice should only be available for really tough issues or very shy people, but it should not be the norm!

Here's the challenge: feedback rules are not universal. Feedback is one of the eight areas, in which cultures differ from each other according to Professor Erin Meyer, author of The Culture Map. In fact, how someone gives and receives feedback differs greatly from culture to culture. So, there is even another hurdle for fostering a feedback culture if your startup team is multicultural.

Nevertheless, there are clear benefits to a good feedback culture and it will definitely pay off so make an effort to establish it in the best way you can.

Keeping in mind that good feedback is not universal and no one really likes it, even less so excels at it, start from scratch and set the rules for the particular feedback culture you want to see in your company and educate and familiarise everyone with it. Think of it as the common ground that everyone is working towards and you all need to get used to it, no matter what the preferences or cultural customs are.

Address the fact of there being cultural differences in feedback rules directly. When people are aware of the fact and mindful about it, they can try to adjust their tone and style of giving feedback as well as their attitude in receiving and dealing with feedback to each other. For example, I have heard a Dutch person say to an Indian colleague: 'We Dutch are very direct and I know that in India, people are rather shy and polite when it comes to saying something rather negative. But I want you to know that it is not at all personal or meant offensively what I want to tell you, but if it comes across too rude or offensive it is because of my culture. I want to give you my honest opinion so we can work on improving our ways of working together.'

Interestingly, what happened next was, our Indian colleague listened to the feedback and then asked the Dutch colleague with honest interest, how a Dutch person would respond and what he should do with this feedback now. The two sat together and outlined a new structure together. That was the most fruitful feedback conversation I personally have ever witnessed.

If you want to know where to start with setting up your feedback culture, start by setting out some common ground rules for everyone in your company regardless of their backgrounds and cultures. Here's our list of the most accepted ones:

For situational and personal feedback:
- Be prepared and willing to actively listen yourself
- Choose the right time and place
- Be specific and focus on what matters
- Don't attack the person only the issue at hand
- Offer solutions and help if possible.

For performance review talks:
- Encourage self-assessment
- Get their view on things and on their own performance
- Remember to give praise and critique
- Encourage change
- Offer solutions and help.

During the onboarding of new team members, do address the fact that there are cultural differences in what is considered good feedback. They don't need to know what differences there are exactly or what to watch out for. Simply being aware and mindful of the fact can avoid misunderstandings and conflict because if an individual feels attacked, they could approach the other person and ask them directly whether this was a cultural thing for them do it this way, just like my Dutch and Indian colleague did.

If your overall company culture is strong and your team is aligned, everyone will assume that everyone means well, so there is no reason to believe that a certain comment or feedback was intended to hurt.

Lastly, remember that feedback is a gift. If you don't appreciate it, you might not get another one. Having a feedback culture means that you respond and act on feedback yourself. Your people need to see that their feedback is valued, so whenever you make a decision or a change based on someone's feedback, then say so.

The Art of Efficient Meetings

Have you ever been in a meeting where you didn't really know what it was about, people wandered in late and took ages to get round to the topic you were there to discuss? You found there were people there who didn't need to be which meant the meeting was too large, you didn't come to any final decisions, and everyone left to rush off to another meeting – where they were likely to go through the whole soul crushing process all over again. We've all been there.

How many times have you shifted other commitments to attend a meeting, missed your lunch and or shelved something really important like your next funding application, only to find that nothing was achieved?

You had totally wasted another hour of your life.

Well, that's life for so many people. That's what most meetings can end up like if you don't have a meeting culture set up from the start and are ruthless about enforcing it.

There are truly choking statistics out there about meetings, and we have seen it with our own eyes as well. Employees lose 30% of their time in meetings, time they could have invested in other productive tasks. In total, ineffective meetings make professionals lose thirty-one hours every month, which works out at roughly four working days.

You are the founder, so it's up to you to make sure meetings aren't like that in your company.

Instead, set up some clear guidelines. You can call them rules if you like, but often people like bending rules or going against them altogether so find a better word if you can. Whatever you call your 'rules', do make sure that people know that they are expected to do things that way in your company.

After all, a culture is simply *The Way We Do Things Around Here*, so you need to set The Way early, and make sure people align with that.

Here's a checklist that might help you. Ask yourself, and expect your team to do the same:

1. Should this really be a meeting?

Whenever you invite someone to a meeting you are interrupting their workflow, consuming their time and keeping them from other tasks. So, always question whether you can spend that time more productively on something else like writing, thinking, testing? Or do you really need that meeting to keep the other things moving both for you and your co-workers?

This question is all about the purpose of the meeting. Why are you meeting? If only to share information, an email will probably do. If you need to be creative together to benefit from the dynamics of the group, go ahead.

Generally, meetings in person are needed for:

■ Decision making
■ Connecting and socialising
■ Brainstorming

They are usually not necessary for:

■ Reporting
■ Informing
■ Briefing
■ Asking for feedback, consent or input
■ Anything which needs a paper trail

2. Are my meeting goals relationship-based or task-based?

If the answer is task-based, such as planning a project, presenting results or briefing your team, then you might be better off using a different channel. Maybe a quick virtual meeting if you expect many questions after the briefing. But most of the time, such task-based contacts can be kept to emails or direct messaging channels, especially, when it would be beneficial to have a paper trail for facts and figures anyway.

If the meeting goal is to strengthen connections, maintain relationships or get an emotional message across, it is usually better to meet in person.

3. Am I prepared for the meeting?

Are you clear on the purpose of the meeting, its objectives, desired outcome and do you have an agenda? Did you invite the right people and only those who really need to be there? How short can this meeting optimally be? Do you have the documentation ready, put all necessary information into the calendar invitation and feel confident to lead the meeting on time, on topic and within the rules?

So, you need a meeting. Now, how should you meet to make it efficient and productive?

At Lilium, we used to have a white board in every meeting room. So I had magnets produced, with **'DESIRED OUTCOME'**, **'AGENDA'** and **'ACTION STEPS'** written on them and put them on the white boards. Whenever there was a meeting, people wrote the respective matter below the magnet, so it was before everyone's eyes throughout the meeting.

It's good practice to minimise wasted time so to get things done: -

  A. Set an **agenda**. Write down which topics you want to discuss and how long you will allow for each point.

  B. Formulate a **desired outcome**. Is it a decision, a solution to a problem or creative input? What should be the result in the end?

C. Designate the **roles**.

D. One person should be the **note taker**, who then circulates the minutes of the meeting afterwards. The minutes of the meeting contain a summary of the most important points discussed, not a transcript, the outcome and further action steps you agreed on. Those need to be clearly assigned to individuals with a clear deadline. You can find a template for Meeting Minutes, which you can copy directly from this book on page 262.

E. Another person is the **time keeper**, who makes sure you start and end on time and keeps an eye on the agenda points and the time.

F. There must be a **chairperson** moderating and leading though the meeting. That person has to guide the conversation according to the agenda points, keep the discussion focused and steer towards the desired outcome.

After the meeting, **follow up on the action steps** and keep everyone accountable for theirs. You've agreed on them together. A helpful one pager version of this chapter for you to print out can be found in the back of this book on page 264.

Top Tip:

Formulate basic meeting rules and write them down. For specifically online meeting rules, see back of this book, page 264. Examples are to be punctual and start and end on time, to come prepared, stay mentally and physically present, listen with an open mind, close decisions and identify next action steps. But they won't be much use on your intranet, so print them on a piece of cardboard – maybe visualised with little icons – and place it on the meeting table with a photo holder or make them a screensaver on your meeting room TV, or have one rule written on every wall as wall tattoo or engraved on the meeting room table... Have fun with it!

How much do meetings cost you?

If you want to get tough on discouraging meetings, just add up a few costs.

You know the salary of each attendee of your meeting. Break them down to a Gross hourly rate and then add them together. Also add on the time needed to catch up on productivity afterwards and factor in the time other people in your company weren't able to proceed with their work because they were waiting for an attendee's response to something else. With 100 people the costs of meetings per year can be terrifying and run into tens of thousands!

Thousands of pounds/euros/dollars might be a good investment if the meetings are all necessary, well organised, productive and driven by results. But, if they aren't, then double the costs to the figures above.

Added to that, team morale goes down, because everyone dreads another meeting and will be demotivated, distracted and unproductive in most meetings as a result. This is a fertile ground for conflicts and miscommunication and can lead to severe friction in the team.

4.4 When Things go Wrong

When you don't put these simple things in place and let people run wild, things can quickly get out of hand. If you think you only need rules or a plan when you have a hundred people or more, think again. One startup that we know of had thirty-two team members and when an external consultant interviewed the team members these were some of their responses.

'Our team meetings are such a waste of time!'

'There's a lack of meeting culture...'

'I have established my own processes and guidelines for my team, the ones for the whole company simply don't make sense for us.'

'There's a lack of cross team communication and a lack of confidence to feed back to the founder that the company guidelines aren't effective...'

'There is this one team member who simply won't speak much and doesn't get involved in anything. I simply let him be, but I think we'll have to let him go eventually.'

'There's a lack of empathy for an introvert'.

'Our manager is just not engaged and isn't really communicating with us. We feel completely cut off from the rest of the company.'

So bad communication can be a personal thing. Every individual is different when it comes to communication. Qualities, such as openness, honesty, courage and a willingness and ability to really listen, vary from person to person. On top of that, we all have good and bad days and bring a lifetime of experience with environments in which conflicts were simply ignored or where telling the truth was even dangerous. These responses show the importance of not just setting up meeting guidelines, but of creating a culture where people can tell you what's not working, without fear of reprisals.

Miscommunication

——— What does bad communication look like? ———

No-one feels responsible for internal communication – but it is a management duty full stop!

If you feel unable, or don't have much time for certain parts of the communication process such as formulating the weekly email, organising the team meeting, collecting all the information from all departments each week for your updates, then make sure you delegate it to someone, whom you can hold accountable for it and support him/her personally.

If you delegate **YOUR** part of the communication function, make sure the whole team respects the nominated person, even if it is just a 30% staff position next to other duties. It won't happen automatically, you need to tell people that they must supply this person with the information as readily as they would supply you with what you need. Hold your leaders and managers accountable for communicating with each other in a way you want them to (rules and tools apply) and to provide you/your communication representative with all the updates you need to communicate further and make decisions.

Here are some common communication errors. Little mistakes and omissions can quickly escalate, so have a read and be warned so you don't fall into any of these bear traps:

1. No, or only insufficient communication – communication is not taken seriously and managed professionally and with the urgency and importance it deserves. Team members find out information about the company from external media or at a later point in time by chance. That's a huge trust buster. Don't do it. Keep people in the loop with important news yourself.

2. Information being held back or distorted. This triggers speculation, interpretation and leads to fear and frustration inside your teams.

3. No co-ordination between management and leaders. This is really toxic and can lead to missing information on each side and shows that the company is not united. When people think that the left hand doesn't know what the right hand is doing, people lose faith and culture starts to take an unpleasant turn for the worse. Classic examples of this include when management announces a great fiscal year in the media, but the team leader is told that there's no money for salary increases due to revenue losses. You can be sure there will be a loss of trust by your team members for a very long time.

4. Wrong timing – make sure your team members always know before the external world. But also, be careful not to communicate something half-baked too early on internally, which has a potential confidentiality breach to the media in mind. In general, a day before going public is a perfect time to inform your internal team members.

5. No dialogue – there are no possibilities to give feedback or to exchange thoughts across departments and across levels.

A good feedback and communication culture needs the right tools such as an anonymous complaint box, communication tools, open door policy, Q&A session after each team meeting plus many more. This has to be established and lived by the management. That's **YOU!** When people do give feedback, make sure you treat it respectfully and take it seriously. Make sure you let everyone know if you can, what you will do about the problem at hand or the particular concern. It's no good just listening if nothing ever changes. People get sceptical very quickly!

6. Not targeting your messages appropriately. Every team member has to be informed about anything which is relevant for them to do their job, remain focussed and feel valued, informed, aligned and motivated. But be selective! Don't flood everyone with information, if you do, the really important messages get lost in the noise.

7. Wrong channels – it is always good to choose two or three channels for very important messages. But even if you choose only one, make sure this reaches 100% of your target group. If this group are the line workers in production where they don't have access to their computers every day, an email might not be the best choice of channel.

8. No appreciative communication – feedback can and must also have the form of acknowledgement of achievements, celebrations and congratulations. A Thank you and a Well done in front of the whole team lifts the spirit, motivates and gives real life examples to everyone of what is considered great work in your company.

Create a culture where success is celebrated and appreciated. That means you need to make a special effort to notice what's working, and not just pick up on what's not working. Stay positive if you want to create a *can-do* culture.

OK, so now you know what you shouldn't do. But both you and your team are only human. Mistakes are going to happen. You will most likely face the situation at least once in your young startup where there is miscommunication, misunderstanding, no clear or complete communication, no communication at all, or simply BAD communication.

You are all growing into your roles – even the CEO, in many cases especially the CEO.

Communication is a learning process.
 So, what can you do if, and when, things go wrong?

Firstly, once you know it's happening, do something about it.
 Communicate the correct message, make it clear that the other message is to be ignored. Apologise if you've accidentally created anguish or stress. Point out that it was a mistake and it's a good thing you have a good error and learning culture, so people will take it as a good example of how to deal with mistakes themselves in the future. At the same time, they will forgive you because you show them that you are learning and trying hard.
 Then, you can make sure to repeat regularly that communication is only official when certain things are given such as during the all hands meetings or via Mail from you direct. Have clear rules about official communication and use only the dedicated tools for it. Make sure everyone knows them and knows they can and should, ask you directly about something they have heard 'through the grapevine'. Make sure they feel like they can come to you with any doubtful or unclear communication before rumours spread and people start interpreting it incorrectly.
 Lastly, find out how this miscommunication arose in the first place and make sure you implement measures to prevent it

from happening again. You need to do things like instruct your leadership team to align with you better before communicating something half baked.

Crisis Communication

It is never more important to get the right message out at the right time via the right channels than during a crisis. This plan will prepare you for an emergency or unexpected event and includes steps to take when a crisis first emerges, which explains how to communicate with the public and how to prevent the issue from occurring again.

Depending on your company's size, location, industry and whether you have a product or offer services, there are various crises which can potentially happen. These could include natural disasters, such as earthquake or flood, cyber-attacks, a virus, a pandemic, employee or management misconduct, leak of privileged information, product failings, faults, or recalls, a fire, sabotage, financial crises such as significant losses, fraud or even bankruptcy. The list goes on, which makes it impossible to propose one set of principles to follow for all companies out there. But the good news is that there are specialised crisis communication consultants and agencies, which can help you set yourself up for the potential time of need. I highly recommend consulting with one. If you're not there yet in terms of being crisis ready, if you are just in the early stages of your company and there just isn't time, don't worry. There's some basics here for you to give you something to fall back on.

Even though this book cannot serve you fully, you definitely need to know that this exists, that it is important and that you need it. If you are prepared for it, there is a pretty good chance you will survive the crisis and maybe even grow stronger out of it by learning from it, as Jody did.

Jody, hired at an early stage as a communication specialist in a software startup, shared her experience of developing a crisis communications Plan of Action with me.

'I had heard about crisis communication during my time at University and I had a notion of how important it was for us to have one in place. I felt it was essential as we had people physically operating and manufacturing machines, which were safety hazards when operated incorrectly. But I had no idea about how I could draw a suitable crisis communication plan up from scratch,' she told me.[6]

So, she asked her network for help and started out small but effectively.

This is what she did:

Step 1: *She drafted the plan itself and structured it into the following sections:*

1. *Purpose: Explaining why the plan is needed and for what exactly. In other words, defining 'What is a crisis?' in simple terms*
2. *Activation: Determining who can activate the plan and when. Which criteria have to be met?*
3. *Procedures: Outlining the steps that are needed to be taken in regard to internal and external communication. Who is responsible for what and which channels should they use whether e-mail, intranet, press release, Twitter or any other?*

Step 2: *Jody convened a designated crisis communication team. This team was responsible for collecting information, creating and disseminating key messages internally and working with the media. They also monitored any response* to the crisis to react if necessary. Every crisis communication team member had a specific role with predefined tasks and duties during a crisis, and every role had a backup person should the designated responsible person be sick or on vacation.

She initiated trainings for a crisis with this team one weekend and thought up some scenarios, like one of the responsible persons or the channel of choice not being available.

Step 3: Jody compiled potential key messages.
She made a list of potential crises her company could face and developed key messages to be used in response. She noted down possible questions from team members as well as the media and drafted responses to those.

Step 4: She prepared the internal communication.
She made a rough plan for how, when and through whom to communicate to the team if a crisis happened. She even had a plan B in case the building, certain channels or internal communications were no longer available. Jody regularly reminded the whole company in their newsletter about their social media policy and that team members must not to talk to the media.

Step 5: She compiled a contacts and media list.
Jody gathered all contact information for local government offices, public health departments, evacuation centres, police and fire departments, Red Cross centres, suppliers and any other organisations she could think of as potentially relevant to communicate with during a crisis.

For the media list, she sorted the contact information by local, national and trade press and marked the most important industry press.

Step 6: *She created Crisis Communication Cards.*
Jody put the important action steps including contact information for each crisis communication team member on a card in the format of a credit card, so it would fit into a regular wallet, handbag or purse.

Important note:

Although the six steps above sound like quite a lot, they are mostly preparation steps you do once and then only update them if necessary. The crisis communication plan itself should be kept short and simple. During a crisis, people need to understand their duties and act quickly. Add the date the document was last edited to ensure people have the latest version. Format the plan in such a way that sections can be detached and each crisis team member can create their own plan of action. Have hard and soft copies in place and require the crisis team members to keep a copy at home or with them at all times in their wallets or bags. During a crisis not everyone will have access to a computer and paper can be carried and copied.

Top Tip:

Once the members of your crisis communication team know the process and what they have to do when and how, you should conduct crisis trainings with them during a weekend. Have a proper debriefing meeting afterwards to discuss what went well and what needs improving or adjusting. For this, start by laying out a fictional scenario, like an office fire, cyber-attack or a case of harassment gone public. Then, hand out paper and pens and ask the team to note down questions, ideas and everything they notice in the process. Don't be surprised if these trainings always take longer than planned or expected, so build in a big buffer and organise lunch for the team. You will need it to re-energise and keep the morale up. Out of experience, though, we recommend working with an external expert at least initially, because there is so much to consider. It is so easy for it to get out of hand that you risk spending a lot of energy and time on the preparation and training, which, when it fails leads to frustration and disappointment. Have a look on the internet, there are many agencies and consultants which can help you – from setting up the process for training yourself to conducting the trainings and analysing the outcome.

Difficult Conversations

In fact, when we want to collaborate, communication is so important that an organisation can be defined as the entirety of communicative relationships.

One founder told me, that although she only has one co-founder at the moment and no team, they still seem to communicate too much. They seem to talk about the same things over and over again but never really come to any final conclusion or decision and the discussion drags on for another day.

With only two people you can still not be communicating efficiently or 'correctly' even though it feels so natural to simply start talking as soon as you see each other in the office in the morning when you both have the same passion and the same goal.

This might come as a surprise to you, but this is exactly what makes it so difficult. When there are only two, three or even four people, conversation simply starts about what you care about.

You really want to help each other and come to a conclusion and really want to make yourself understood and understand the other or so it seems. But conversation is exactly the word, which should ring all the alarm bells!

If you are talking business with your co-founder, then inform, brief, ask, decide. Communicate, but be careful you don't just 'chat things through'.

When you need to talk about a certain issue, make it official, schedule a meeting with rules, with an agenda, a desired outcome and a limited time dedicated to it. After that, don't discuss any further but schedule another official meeting for it if necessary.

It might sound and feel silly for just the two of you, especially if you're sitting next to each other all day long. But try to avoid that topic for the rest of the day. After a while you will see, 'officialising' that topic with a meeting will have made your discussion more productive and efficient because it is not a conversation anymore but an official business matter.

Difficult conversations aren't just limited to warnings, bad feedback or letting go of one of your team members. Difficult conversations can occur anytime and with anyone – investors, partners, customers, team members, family.

Keep an open mind and an open ear and whatever you do, stay calm, professional and solution-oriented.

First things first. Everyone feels awkward having a difficult conversation. That's why they're called difficult conversations!

But here's the thing, now you have chosen the path to lead, it's part of your job to have them. You need to set boundaries and rules, feel the consequences when people overstep the mark and act on them, so they don't happen again.

It might mean you have to let go of a friend because they didn't fit in with the culture or simply wasn't performing as expected. It can mean giving someone a warning or bad feedback about an unwanted behaviour. It can mean informing your investors about a negative development or incident. Whatever it may be, you need to be prepared.

To really give you guidance on this topic would exceed the scope of this book, but we wanted to encourage you with the following things you can do:

1. Ask advice from other founders, leaders and people you look up to.

2. Find a specialised mentor who is good at dealing with difficult situations.

3. Get some training and role play different scenarios ahead of time.

4. Sign up for a training for difficult conversations and grow into your leader role.

You might think now, 'That's it? No more advice? Best practice? No more tips or stories?' But believe me, these four bullet points – as simple and innocent as they may sound – are heavily loaded with advice and best practice out of our own experience and are not to be taken lightly. In fact, following them is a very profound and meaningful thing to do.

4.5 Scaling – As You Grow

Keeping the Knowledge

If you are at the early stages of your startup and are still a micro team, then knowledge tends to flow easily between people. But it doesn't take very long with just one or two additional team members before things start getting lost and the cracks start to show. This section is about what to do when either you need to scale up to a bigger team, or you start growing a remote team or you have a turnover of people and knowledge gets lost.

If you aren't at the growth stage yet, you might still want to get a heads up with what you might face later so you feel prepared and know what signs to look out for which tell you when you might need to start putting some systems in place.

There are two things you will need to capture and preserve – knowledge and expertise. They are different.

You need to capture *knowledge*, whatever stage of growth you are at. You do this by collecting content such as documents, information flows like emails, your customer management software or notes on your system about customers/suppliers/ investors. It's everyone's responsibility to do their share of record keeping and you need to set the standard and make it clear that it's part of everyone's job to keep good records. You are the leader, so you need to set the example!

You keep expertise by *keeping* people.

You can share knowledge by making people share it in tools. You can share expertise by encouraging people to share it with others.

A typical scenario that I saw happen was the chaos caused by someone leaving who hadn't kept good records. The team was in a meeting discussing the new requirements of an existing client that had been handed over to a new account manager. They didn't have any information about the current requirements and couldn't work out what had to be adjusted. The new account manager had to ask the client for the old specs and the client had to dig around to find it. This happened twice. The client got cross. The new account manager failed to prepare a presentation and invite the client over to show progress on their project, which was the unofficial procedure of the previous account manager but no one knew about it. The client ended the contract.

This is one of dozens of stories I know about not having knowledge and expertise management in place.

Now think about your company, you might not have clients yet if you are just getting going, your team might be still bringing things to market, but it doesn't take long before informal communication becomes something that leaves gaps in your company. So always be thinking ahead about what's important to keep abreast of.

Knowledge Management

For knowledge to be managed you need two things: firstly, an intranet or a document storage tool, where you can store all that knowledge and secondly, the people who actually write it down, share it and keep it up to date. The latter is the tricky part since no one feels responsible and no one has or makes time for it as it is not considered part of their daily job.

You can change that.

If everyone is involved and knows about it, they will also tend to look up information in this centralised area of your document system.

You should also collect all official regulations, requirements, norms and industry standards as well as your official company policies, rules and processes in this place. And if you, or the management is being asked where to find knowledge or information about anything, instruct your leadership team to not supply the information, but tell them they can find it in the official knowledge base. This way, you make sure they have to use it so they will know what and where they can find everything they need from then on. They will also find out what might still be missing and either contribute that themselves or ask for it to be added, which helps you manage the knowledge and information and keep it all up to date.

Make sure, the structure is clear, logical, easy to find and searchable. It also helps to make it a well thought out page or structure on a professional intranet or knowledge base tool. There's been such an explosion of cloud-based tools recently, that there's no excuse for not having a central place where people can find what they need. Just make sure that people are all using the same system! Project management tools that incorporate project channels or folders that are searchable, where you can upload, store and search for important documents are easy to find and cheap to implement. Take a look at systems like Asana, Slack, Wrike, ClickUp and many others which will help you keep everything in one place and reduce the number of emails going back and forth.

Top Tip:

How do you avoid people logging on, not finding what they think is a relevant folder and creating more folders so it soon becomes a mass of folders each with only one or two items in? Make it part of their job description, introduce 'knowledge-time' – this is a dedicated half hour slot every Friday in which everyone should reflect on what knowledge they have gained over the past week or have from previous employment and should share – and then actually do it. Reinforce it or better yet, reward good work with a free lunch voucher every month for the best knowledge-time article for example.

Perhaps have a folder which all new items go into and a designated person who files them each week? Or perhaps a designated person from each department such as Marketing, IT, R&D, HR, Finance etc. would have a folder in the department area, which they have responsibility for. People feed in ideas to the relevant department's folder and the designated department person files it. You'll also need to vet them as ideas in case they simply don't work. The designated people could all liaise with the naming format so it is relevant. Or each department discusses amongst themselves and agree their own naming format.

It has to work for everyone.

Expertise Management

Unlike knowledge, hard facts and information, skills and expertise are harder – if not impossible to write down. Create a culture of shared expertise and internal mentoring. Encourage everyone to make internal internships, volunteer in other areas of the business or simply ask for advice to show them how something can be done.

Being a mentor should come with some advantages which will motivate people to make time for it and share their skills and expertise. For example, there could be a 'mentor of the year'- award at your summer party or mentees can vote for a mentor to receive a book voucher. Or there can be some sort of gamification where people can collect badges for certain achievements or accomplishments, such as the sustainability badge for anyone who helps clean up the office, turns off the lights after everyone has left, comes to work by bike etc. or simply the expertise or expert's badge.

If you want your people to share their expertise and show their skills, which teaches others, you could organise 'expert sessions' in the form of workshops, presentations, Q&A sessions where anyone in the company could share their expertise with others in a voluntary and informal way. Organising this can cost you a bit more in overheads but it's worth it to promote and encourage the sharing of expertise as well as engage and connect people. Assuming you have people's consent, you could film these sessions and put them on your intranet or later, on your learning platform, should you plan to have one in the future. They can be the practical part of your 'Company Academy'.

Documentation

It's not exciting, but it's important!

We have already talked about the importance of having a set of ground rules early on in your startup in the chapter on Recruitment, which can grow as you need them to. Our experience shows that it is of such a great importance that we want to lay it out once more under the perspective of communication.

To summarise:

As you grow, introduce company polices and processes as previously discussed. For more detail go back and look at the relevant section in the Recruitment chapter. Put simply the benefits of putting basic rules, processes and policies into writing and making them official and obligatory to follow in your company are clear:

1. They create an atmosphere where team members are treated equally and with respect.

2. People have a clear perspective and sense of how to behave, what to do and how.

3. The consequences for not complying are clear, known and not random.

4. They encourage open communication between you and your team members.

5. They automate, thus speed things up as the ways to do something do not need to be discussed or developed for every new situation.

6. They ensure that knowledge and information is kept within the company in a way that everyone can find easily, can access and use properly.

Communication Strategy

Your communication strategy relies highly on your company's mission and values and includes the types and channels of communication. It is the very centre piece of how, when and why you interact with your team members.

Basically, the strategy is the overall WHAT, while a concrete plan derived from the strategy, shows the HOW by serving as a roadmap. Your roadmap will need to be adjusted over time. The most important thing to remember is that you cannot communicate too much!

There's nothing that alienates people more than feeling they don't know what's going on.

How do you develop your strategy?

To be frank, in the beginning you don't really need an internal communication strategy. If you have a rough idea of what your communication culture should look like and take deliberate actions towards establishing and nurturing it, you will be perfectly fine for some time. But if you feel like it's time to scale up, do read on.

From personal experience, it will take you up to two working days to organise and create the first raw strategy for the initial internal communication process for your team. You might have to adjust it here and there once it is out there and you will need to consider the time you continuously take to manage the channels, keep the quality of content for the meetings up, create more content and communicate it. But these little measures are very fruitful when scaling. After six months, you should create a short survey to get written feedback on your communication and culture to get a feel for any adjustments and to check whether you are on the right track.

If you're curious, here is how such an internal communication strategy and plan could look like.

1

WHY?

Their company's vision, mission, and goals.

2

WHAT?

The communication goal and key messages for the next six months.

3

FOR WHOM?

A description of the audience – considering cultural and professional backgrounds, age, gender, etc.

4

WHERE?

A list of all available channels and types of communication to be used in the beginning plus a rough guideline on tone and wording.

5

WHEN?

The planned frequency of communication (including milestones and events).

6

WHO?

An overview of who is responsible
for delivering communication.

7

HOW?

Ideas for measurements of success
for constant evaluation.

In conclusion, there are costs associated with communicating, but there are even bigger costs associated with not communicating enough or communicating badly.

Alumni and Staff Leavers

Jennifer's story

When Jennifer had her last day at work before leaving for maternity leave, she was excited and happy. Her colleagues had organised a lovely Baby-shower/farewell-party and she felt appreciated, loved and missed already.

On that day, she had no idea that this feeling would shortly change. During her maternity leave, she only heard news and updates about the company from the media or from close colleagues by chance. She thought that they (they being her direct manager, her team, the founders, the management, or HR) were being considerate and didn't want to bother or bore her with work matters. But when she contacted her manager shortly before returning to work, he told her that there had been a change in the structure which meant he was no longer her manager. So, she contacted her new manager, who was surprised that she was going to return so soon. But he tried to welcome her back and help her feel part of the new team.

Unfortunately, this communication faux-pas left Jennifer feeling she was no longer valued which she tried to ignore. She soon realised that working part time meant that she could no longer take part in afternoon meetings, and her team only filled her in if she asked proactively. When she asked her manager if they could move meetings to the mornings, he told her that the meetings were not necessary for her as they didn't impact on her job directly. She was no longer included in any strategic or bigger projects, since her manager wanted to make the best use of her limited time at work. She ended up doing the work of an intern which demoralised her to the extent she started to think about quitting.

We've already talked about the importance of staying in touch with your ex team members or alumni as it strengthens the culture inside your company. We gave you various ideas and ways in which you can do that.

Once you grow and start to mature as a company, there is another group of people that you need to think about. Eventually, there will be people on long-term sick leave, parental leave, or sabbaticals.

You can see from Jennifer's experience, that this type of internal communication can make or break a relationship with knowledgeable, skilled, motivated and loyal people. Just because someone has been gone for a while and maybe only returns part time this does not mean they are less capable and less willing to contribute and bring your cause forward. In fact, quite the opposite.

With Jennifer and many young mothers and fathers we have talked to over the years, we have heard a common theme. After a longer absence from work, taking care of household and family, they are more excited and motivated to finally come back and use their wits and brains again. Caring for a baby, a household and a family is indeed a strenuous, demanding, yet fulfilling full-time job, but it is a different type of job altogether. Becoming a parent doesn't mean you want a career change!

People on long-term sick leave are often thrilled to finally come back to work and live the life they had when they were thriving, productive, feeling useful and part of something bigger.

Neglecting those people would be a mistake, especially if your company culture claims to be family friendly and human centric.

You might have to adjust certain things in the beginning, like additional overhead for the internal communication to these groups of people, rescheduling afternoon meetings for those working part time, hiring temporary staff to fill in during absence or for the other part of the part time job or even finding some other member of staff to job share. But part time will usually come to an end, motivation will increase and loyalty will pay off.

Top Tip:

Don't overcomplicate things. It will go a long way already if your HR team keeps in touch with leavers and forwards important and relevant information to them. They can keep lists of all leavers and send out emails in the form of newsletters. This should be done in any way suitable for – and agreed upon by – both parties.

Your Communication Wrap Up

- **Introduce a single source of truth** with one channel where people get all the official news and information – and in good time.

- **Mind different cultures.** Keep your audience in mind.

- **The goal of any communication** should be to inform, align, connect and/or motivate.

- **Develop a coherent and consistent communication culture** set the tone, show by example and enforce how you want your team to communicate and collaborate.

- **For a full remote or hybrid workplace** – many of the rules will be the same, but there are nuances on how to deliver.

- **Don't overdo it,** make it short, simple and clear. Better done than aiming for perfection and not finishing. Try, fail, learn and adjust.

EPILOGUE

Please find in this chapter, templates, checklists, processes and first steps which we have gathered together to help you further.

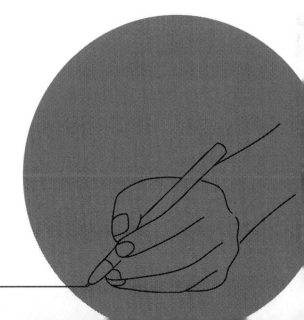

Both of us have consulted and worked in lots of different startups with experience of both early stage startups, and some who were a few years into their journey.

When you are lucky enough to work with a large number companies, you can see the patterns and similarities.

The common challenges of founders, teams and cultures in these early companies run through almost every startup we have had the privilege to work with.

In almost every case, the founders had prepared the ground well; they had done thorough market research, verified their service/product in terms of existing patents, market requirements and demands. Most had screened competitors and the market itself, written a business plan, done the legal work to create their company and produced a prototype.

They had found a freelance designer, who had created their brand and started to do social media marketing, in some cases they hired someone to do this for them. They had found investors or raised money through crowdfunding, signed contracts with suppliers and partners and maybe even already launched their service/product. But when the time came to build up a team, they either jumped in unprepared or – much less often – persisted in ignorance.

We realised that regardless of the stage of the company, or industry, the problems these companies faced so often came down to people and culture. And their challenges were always remarkably similar.

Most of these founders were isolated and stuck, feeling alone inside the bubble of their company with their problem. That's especially true in the early days. All too often people have nobody to turn to as the people and communications side challenges take them by surprise. Founders often struggle to find the time or realise that their personal strengths aren't good when dealing with people, communication and culture.

When you don't see it as a specialised area yourself, it really does come as a surprise when it doesn't take care of itself!

If you feel like that, trust us, you are not alone.

You cannot be an expert or know everything. Just be aware of what you need to take care of, know how to help yourself and know where to get help when you do need it.

One day, we received an email from one of our newest mentees, which confirmed what we had thought for a while, that there is a real need to create a compilation of experiences and tips for founders so that they can develop a better understanding of the people side in business.

We know by talking to experts, founders and from our own experience, that if founders start to include the people strategy as an integral part of the overall business strategy they will end up with a much more well-rounded business plan and will, therefore, be much more likely to succeed.

With permission of our mentee C., we wanted to share with you what led us here.

From: C
To: MM & MS
Date: 20 January 2000

Dear M.,
I am very much looking forward to our mentoring sessions over the next couple of months. I am grateful for this opportunity of a mentorship in team and culture development since there are so many points to be considered like Recruiting, HR, Communication, Purpose,

Vision, Mission, Leadership and so on, which are clearly not my strong points. I did some research and took notes but I have to admit that it is still a blurry mess in my head. I hope you don't mind me sending you my most pressing questions in advance, which I would like to get answers to during our mentoring programme:

- *Where do I find the best employees?*
- *How do I define the salary?*
- *How do I conduct an interview?*
- *How do I keep employees in my company?*
- *What are my next steps concretely?*

I hope you are OK with that and once again thank you for your time and effort!

Best Regards,

C.

This led to us to writing this book to share knowledge, answer questions and create profound guidance so founders know how to help themselves and find a way to deal with issues when they arise, and they will. They always do in startups.

This is just the beginning of your journey. Enjoy the ride and make sure your team rides right beside you!

Top Tips summary:

We asked people from our network of founders from different industries around the world, what their top piece of advice to a fresh founder would be. We think it will help to share their valuable answers with you. We handpicked the most important and most intriguing ones so you can copy them and pin them next to your desk.

- Don't overthink; try out ideas, fail and try something else until you succeed. That is what a STARTup is for. Also, start with an MVP (minimal viable product).

- Trust your gut feeling, follow your instincts and listen to your intuition.

- 'Hire slow and fire fast' (original quote from Sarah Blakely)

- Trust yourself, believe in yourself, but remain open for critique, challenge and suggestions from others. Find a healthy balance.

- Start developing your team from day one and insist on a good data management system.

- In the beginning, cultural fit with core skills and potential to grow is most important in your employees.

- Always focus on the solution, not on the problem. #solution-oriented mindset!

- Make decisions and stand by them. Be patient but persistent.

- The right co-founders are elementary for your company. Find those who want to invest 100% of their energy.

THE FIRST STEPS EVERY FOUNDER NEEDS TO BE SUCCESSFUL

Step 1: Identify your core culture – mission, vision, purpose and values

Step 2: Activate your long-term thinking muscle – ideas are your bread and butter. Emphasise productivity in the early days to ensure your company doesn't drown in its initial workload.

Step 3: Find the right team – ask what skills you need. Search for like-minded people, but encourage diverse outside-the-box thinking.

Step 4: Put your vocabulary into action – involve your core team into bringing your planned culture to life.

Step 5: Set the path and the pace – provide focus, passion and accountability, foster a solution-oriented mindset.

Step 6: Keep talking to each other – the magic word is team alignment.

Step 7: Introduce simple rules and initial tools – rules about information storage, collaboration, responsibilities, meeting and feedback rules, and tools like Google Drive, Dropbox, Mentimeter, Toggl, Slack, or Mailchimp.

Step 8: Take precautions against burnout – running a startup is like running a marathon. If your team hits a low, it will take your leadership to remotivate them.

Sidestep: Get support – coaches for support/solutions, mentors for expertise, trainers for strategy, consultants for information. Each one is suited to specific help and can provide assistance in different ways.

INTERVIEW PROCESS

Steps for a successful, swift interview process

Keep your processes within 1-2 months from start to offer

1. Assemble interview team between 4-6 people

2. Brief interview team on the job and the interviewers responsibilities and agree to interview steps and length

3. Conduct professional interviews onsite or via video

4. Conduct test with candidates (if applicable)

5. Debrief with interview team and make a decision to offer, reject candidates

6. Make offer to successful candidates Recruiter / Hiring Manager and answer all questions within 1 week

7. Move to contract signature stage and ask contract to be returned within 1 week

DO'S AND DON'TS DURING AN INTERVIEW

Do's

Check the room beforehand, be on time, ask the candidate if he wants a drink/is comfortable on video

Take notes on your laptop and tell the candidate that you will make notes on your laptop as we are a paperless company

Be prepared and explain the interview agenda and layout at the beginning

Maintain good eye contact, sit up straight, lean in slightly from time to time, mirror the candidate's behaviour, keep your arms and legs uncrossed, find a place for your hands, smile, walk with purpose and energy, be graceful, address everyone in the room

Don'ts

Unprepared and dirty meeting room, no fresh air for a while

Texting, answering phone calls or e-mails, checking your phone every 5 minutes or walking out of the room for no reason

Not knowing the job description, requirements or any details about the candidates CV

Bad posture, breaking eye contact, staring, crossed arms, excessive nodding, fidgeting, hands behind the back, mismatched expressions and tone of voice, going to the toilet

*Questions you **should not ask** are around specifics such as:* age, race, ethinicty, colour, gender, gender identity, sexual orientation, family (planning), disability and country of origin.

ONBOARDING CHECKLIST

Pre-boarding: Begin the introduction

- ☐ Wecome email from key teammates
- ☐ New employee announcement email
- ☐ All necessary new hire paperwork delivered
- ☐ Devices selected and prepared for delivery
- ☐ Introduce to mentor

Day 1: Streamline the paperwork process

- ☐ Welcome session with new team
- ☐ Device setup, and IT support
- ☐ Paperwork completed
- ☐ New employee added to necessary collaboration channels and distribution lists
- ☐ New employee swag package (T-shirt, coffee mug etc)

  For on-premise emplyees:
- ☐ Security badge and parking pass provided, if necessary
- ☐ Facilities tour (office space, meeting rooms, cafeteria, gym, etc)

Week 1: Get everyone up to speed

- ☐ Onboarding feedback survey
- ☐ First weekly meeting with mentor(s)
- ☐ Benefits package walkthrough
- ☐ Employee handbook delivered

Month 1: Allow new hires to fly

- ☐ Introduction to team leads
- ☐ Introductory side project assignment
- ☐ One-month check in with managers
- ☐ Team happy hour or lunch

EXIT INTERVIEW TEMPLATE

This document will allow you to gather the most important information and will allow for conversation with your employee who is about to exit your company. Use these questions and make yourself a template by inserting blank spaces after each question to be filled out by the leaver.

EMPLOYEE'S DETAILS

Name:

Current position:

Department:

Start date:

Termination date:

Date of exit interview:

Exit interviewer:

Job description and duties:
- What did you like most and least about your job and why?
- Do you feel that the job description given to you when you took the job accurately describes the role?
- Did you feel valued in your role?
- Did you feel that you had an acceptable workload or were you under- or overworked?

Relationships with line manager and colleagues:
- How would you describe morale in your department?
- How would you describe your working relationship with your colleagues?

How would you describe your working relationship with your line manager?
- Were you treated fairly?
- Did you receive constructive feedback?
- Were you kept informed on company related changes?

Communication:
- How did you feel about the level of communication within your team/department?
- Were the company's overall goals clearly communicated?
- Do you have any suggestions as to how communication at the different levels could be improved?

Compensation and work-life balance:
- Did you feel that you were compensated well?
- Did you feel that you were able to ask for a more flexible working setup (working part time, working remote)? If so, who did you ask?
- If you could have improved anything, what would it have been?

OFFBOARDING CHECKLIST

Prepare Paperwork

- [ ] 401 (k) information
- [ ] Health check information
- [ ] Non-disclosure agreement
- [ ] Non-competent agreements
- [ ] Tax documents
- [ ] Outstanding reimbursements

Knowledge Transfer

- [ ] List of important contacts
- [ ] Useful resources
- [ ] Location of records
- [ ] Status report of ongoing projects
- [ ] List of outstanding tasks

Recover Company Assets

- [ ] IT eqipment
- [ ] Mobile phone
- [ ] ID cards or badges
- [ ] Parking tags
- [ ] Uniforms
- [ ] Access card or keys

IT Permissions and Access

- [ ] Update passwords
- [ ] Revoke employee's access
- [ ] Remove employee from payroll
- [ ] Update directory and org chart
- [ ] Update company website
- [ ] Redirect calls and emails

Exit Interview

- [ ] Exit Interview questionnaire
- [ ] Have discussions after survey
- [ ] Analyze the data collected
- [ ] Retrieve insights

MEETING MINUTES

Meeting/Project Name:	
Date of Meeting:	Start & End Time:
Chair:	Minute Taker:

1. Meeting Objective(s)

Copy these across from the agenda before the meeting.

2. Attendence

Present	Apologies

3. Agenda, Decisions, Issues

Topic/Discussion notes

Add more rows as necessary – put in topics from agenda before the meeting

4. Action Items

Action	Responsible	Due Date

5. CC'd for Information

THE ART OF EFFICIENT MEETINGS

BEFORE THE MEETING

Meeting necessary?
Meetings are good for:
Decision making, social connection and creative interaction/brainstorming

Objectives
What's the goal? Decision, a relationship cultivated or creatively brainstormed?

Agenda
Topics and timings?

Attendees
Minimum number required, others CC'd

Invitations
All information needed to prepare.

Prepare room/call
Is everything available and does everything work?

DURING THE MEETING

Meeting rules
Punctual start and end
Mobile phone ban
No private talk
Let others speak
No personal attacks

Distribute roles
Chairperson (for moderation, rules enforcement etc.)
Timekeeper (for time allocation and punctuality)
Note taker (for the most important points) (see template Meeting Minutes)

Summary
Results, agreed action steps, responsibilities, and deadlines

AFTER THE MEETING

Minutes of the meeting
Send to participants and to anyone who should be informed

Follow up
with those responsible for the next action steps, need help? Can the agreed deadlines be met?

Feedback
Give and receive to learn and keep optimizing

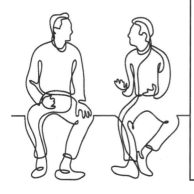

ONLINE MEETING RULES

Find a quiet spot

Camera on

Dress appropriately

Mute your microphone

Raise your hand to speak

Be on time and come prepared

No TV, phone checking, or other distractions

No food

No animals on screen

No speaking when it's not your turn

Don't interrupt

About the Authors

Margareta Sailer and Mareike Mutzberg met when they worked together during the startup phase at Lilium, a unicorn aviation scale-up. Lilium's all-electric vertical take-off and landing passenger aircraft has made it one of the most exciting, highly capitalised, game changing companies in Europe. Their team of highly skilled and passionate people are on a journey to change the future of passenger transport.

Mareike Mutzberg

Mareike Mutzberg was employee number four at Lilium. Initially responsible for setting up and implementing Lilium's internal and external communications & marketing, she became responsible for the culture and employee experience of its rapidly growing team. She has worked for international world-class communication agencies and brings years of experience as mentor and a specialist consultant for think tanks in the areas of Intercultural Competence, Corporate Culture and Communications.

www.mareike-mutzberg.de
www.linkedin.com/in/mareike-mutzberg

Margareta Sailer

Margareta Sailer was key to the people strategy at Tesla, one of the boldest and most successful brands of the 21st Century. As Senior Manager Recruitment for Tesla in Europe, she was responsible for hiring great people. There were thirty people there when she started, and over 4,000 by the end of her tenure, 14,000+ worldwide. Her unique insights into what it takes to hire, inspire and lead come first-hand from key roles at Tesla, Lilium, Leko Labs, HP and RIM/Blackberry. Margareta was an integral part to build the people strategy and structure at Lilium as Global Head of Recruitment most recently, from the ground up.

www.mondaysquares.com
www.linkedin.com/in/margaretasailer

Their consultancy practices are geared to enable founders and organisations to create culture and people strategies to maximise potential and growth.

Notification

In this book you will find the authors' own, personal, reflections and experiences, as Head of Recruitment respectively Culture and Communication Manager of Lilium especially during the early years of Lilium, 2016 to 2018. The same applies to the hyper growth phase and expansion of Tesla, as Senior Manager, Recruitment between May 2010 and September 2015.

Lilium and Tesla do not endorse any of these experiences. The experiences shared in this book reflect the author's own reflections during the period of 2016 and 2018 when Lilium was four to 300+ employees and was going through a prototype development phase. The same applies for the expansion phase of Tesla growing from a company with 300 people worldwide, into the thousands whilst establishing premises across several countries.

Note of Gratitude

We wish to thank the people who have been involved & contributed to this book.

Our gratitude and appreciation to those who support us and believe that people, purpose & success go hand in hand is beyond measure.

To all of our family and friends who cheered us on, every step of the way and through the development of this book. You never fail to keep our motivation, spirits and culture up – thank you.

A special note of gratitude goes to Tom Little who introduced us to Pat Shepherd and her team. Her wisdom and years of experience in writing and publishing books allowed us to reach beyond, learn and stretch ourselves. A special thanks to Cristina Castro, Paula Leach, Elin Hauge, Winifried Johansen and Sophie Bennett.

Sophie, the author of Find your Flame and Money Bondage has been a crucial part of our success, working in tandem with Pat and her team to get us the finished end-result of this book.

Boryana Straubel – A Tribute
Sadly, on the 19th of July 2021, Boryana was involved in a fatal car accident and leaves behind a wonderful family, friends and business partners.

Boryana was the best of all of us. She inspired a generation and lifted our souls. We are forever grateful that we had the opportunity to capture Boryana's wisdom for this book, and that we are able to share it with the consent of the Straubel and Dinev families.

Boryana was founder and CEO of Generation Collection, a sustainable investment jewellery brand as well as Executive Director of the Straubel Foundation, focussing on impact investments that accelerate the transition to a more environmentally sustainable future. Her busy life included roles as an impact fund advisor, a guest lecturer at Stanford as well as being a Presidential Leadership scholar. Boryana sat on several councils sharing her vast experience at Tesla and Wikipedia.

Boryana held two Masters from Stanford University, one in Management Science and Engineering and one in MSx Business, as well as a B.A degree in Economics from University of California, Berkeley.

Arnnon Geshuri

Arnnon holds the position of Chief People Officer of Teladoc Health, the virtual care leader that is transforming how people access healthcare around the world.

Arnnon previously served as the Vice President of Human Resources (CHRO) at Tesla where he oversaw the growth of Tesla from a 400-person startup to an industry leader with more than 35,000 employees around the globe. Prior to Tesla, he was the Senior Director of Staffing Operations and People for Google, where he designed the company's legendary recruitment organisation and talent acquisition strategy. He joined Google in 2004 helping to scale the company from 2,500 employees up to a 25,000 person technology powerhouse.

A true visionary and leader who is dedicated to making this world a better place, Arnnon operates with the highest level of professionalism and integrity which translates into everything he does.

Lisa Bodell

FutureThink CEO Lisa Bodell ranks among the **Top 50 Speakers Worldwide** and is the best-selling author of *Kill the Company* and *Why Simple Wins*. She's a global leader on simplification, productivity, and innovation, whose keynotes leave audiences inspired to change and arms them with radically simple tools to get to the work that matters.

A thought leader and serial entrepreneur, Lisa's transformational message has inspired executives at top-ranked organisations such as Google, Cisco, Citigroup, and the U.S. Navy War College.

Lisa served on the board of advisors of several organisations, and her insights on productivity, simplification and innovation were invaluable to us.

Bettina Andresen Guimarães

Bettina has spent decades within the automotive industry as Director of Communications for Citroën Austria as well as Head of international Communications for Citroën/DS, based in France.

She is a Senior Consultant for Simitri Group International, and runs her own business Authentic Wow. With her Business, Bettina focusses on leadership and intercultural coaching.

With an education in NLP-Resonance®, Corporate and Executive Coaching and Intercultural Communication, she brings a wealth of experience to the table with her twenty-six years of corporate experience in communication.

Communication is a vital part to any company, at any size. Bettina has been instrumental in sharing her wisdom with us for this book.

Paula Leach

Paula spent the first eighteen years of her career as an HR professional at the Ford Motor Company and worked and lived three years in the USA. Later, Paula joined the UK Home Office where she performed different roles as HR Director for Leadership, People Strategy and Change which enabled her to step into the role of Chief People Officer in 2016.

Paula served as Global CPO at the high growth technology company FDM Group until 2020. She created Vantage Point Consulting in early 2021, a mission to help high achievers to make more impact through authenticity, creativity and freedom. She is the author of *Vantage Points*, a book that will inspire you to create a culture where employees thrive.

Paula is FCIPD qualified and received a first class honours Business degree at the Heriot-Watt university as well as an MBA from Henley Business School.

Paula brings a wealth of experience with her and is a true leader.

Winifred Patricia Johansen

Winifred Johansen is the senior vice-president for commercial affairs for Quantafuel ASA, and Chair of the Board of Quantafuel Skive ApS Denmark. She is an engineer, business strategist and leadership researcher.

She has supported several startups over the years and acts as Chair of Ocean Oasis. She has a passion for change and sustainability.

Winifred holds an M.Sc. in Mechanical Engineering from the Norwegian University of Science and Technology (NTNU) and Politecnico di Milano, an MBA from the Robert Gordon University, Aberdeen, and is currently an extramural doctorate researcher on Crisis Sensemaking at the University of Bradford.

Winifred never ceases to amaze us with her curiosity, open mind and relentless energy.

Prof. Claas Triebel

Prof. Claas Triebel is a German psychologist and renowned expert for competence development. During his career, he developed a renowned and awarded Method for Balance of Skills (German: Kompetenzenbilanz). Since 2020, he has been a lecturer at the German Academy of Applied Sciences for Economy and Management in Essen and holds a lectureship at several Academies.

He is also a serial entrepreneur. He recently developed a multi-cultural German speaking network of career coaches and is a consultant for startups and rapidly growing companies with twenty years of experience. He partners with Ralph Suda at the Growth Academy GmbH.

As an author of German non-fiction books in the area of development, career, negotiation and coaching, he was the perfect partner for us.

Ralph Suda
Ralph is a coach, mentor, speaker, serial entrepreneur, business angel and expert for leadership and team development. Ralph is a force of nature who doesn't just crack us up when we speak with him, he knows how to mesmerise audiences due to his successful stand-up comedian, musician and acting background.

His latest venture, the Growth Academy, is focused entirely on the area of team and competence development and serves startups, scaleups and corporates.

Dr. Georg Wolfgang
Munich born, founder and CEO of Culturizer GmbH. Georg has contributed to this book with his wealth of experience and studies in Management and Law. He changes the world, by working with companies and students as lecturer on the topic of organisational behaviour at the Management Centre in Innsbruck, Austria.

Bibliography

Books that inspired us

Big Heart Ventures – Dr. Tina Ruseva
Super Coach – Michael Neill
IKIGAI – Hector Garcia and Frances Miralles
Reimagine Capitalism in a world on Fire – Rebecca Henderson
Climate Justice – Mary Robinson
Believe IT – Jamie Kern Lima
Mission Control Management – Paul Sean Hill
Start with why – Simon Sinek
Leaders at last – Simon Sinek
Homo Deus – *a Brief History of Human Hing and a Brief History of Tomorrow* – Yuval Noah Harari
Think Again – Adam Grant

Footnote references which appear in the book

1. https://www.randstad.co.uk/s3fs-media/uk/public/2020-10/
   UK_REBR2020.pdf
   (p. 100)

2. https://www.linkedin.com/pulse/leadership-attitude-mindset-
   action-andresen-guimarães-née-petz-/
   (p. 139)

3. https://www.linkedin.com/pulse/influence-gender-
   communication-style-debbie-churgai/
   (p. 190)

4. https://www.adhddd.com/comics/)
   (p. 211)
5. https://review.firstround.com/the-founders-guide-to-
   discipline-lessons-from-fronts-mathilde-collin
   (p. 213)

6. https://www.interne-kommunikation.info/definition-interne-
   kommunikation/)
   (p. 233)